Access for Windows® 95
Made Simple

Moira Stephen

MADE SIMPLE
BOOKS

Made Simple
An imprint of Butterworth-Heinemann
Linacre House, Jordan Hill, Oxford OX2 8DP
225 Wildwood Avenue, Woburn, MA 01801-2041
A division of Reed Educational and Professional Publishing Ltd

ℛ   A member of the Reed Elsevier plc group

OXFORD   BOSTON   JOHANNESBURG
MELBOURNE   NEW DELHI   SINGAPORE

First edition published 1996
Reprinted 1997 (twice), 1998 (twice)

© Moira Stephen 1996

TRADEMARKS/REGISTERED TRADEMARKS
Computer hardware and software brand names mentioned in this book are protected
by their respective trademarks and are acknowledged.

British Library Cataloguing in Publication Data
A catalogue record for this book is available from the British Library

ISBN 0 7506 2818 9

Typeset by P.K.McBride, Southampton

Archtype, Bash Casual, Cotswold and Gravity fonts from Advanced Graphics Ltd
Icons designed by Sarah Ward © 1994
Printed and bound in Great Britain by Scotprint, Musselburgh, Scotland

Contents

Preface IX

1   Getting started   1

What is a database? 2

Access objects 4

Preparing your data 6

Getting into Access 8

The Access screen 9

Summary 10

2   Help   11

Contents tab 12

Instant Help 15

Index tab 16

Find tab 18

Answer Wizard 20

Summary 22

3   Building a database   23

Creating a new database 24

Creating a new table 26

Table design window 28

AutoNumber field 30

Date/Time fields 33

Text field 36

Yes/No field 38

Number field 40

Memo field 42

Primary key 43

Saving the design 44

Summary 46

4	Relationships	47

Adding a new table 48

Relationships 49

Making the relationship 50

Table Wizard 52

Checking relationships 56

Closing a database 59

Summary 60

5	Data entry and edit	61

Opening a database 62

Opening a table 63

Using Datasheet view 64

Adding/deleting records 66

Using Form view 68

Summary 70

6	Redesigning a table	71

Adding a field 72

Deleting a field 74

Changing field properties 75

Primary key and indexes 76

Summary.. 78

7   Datasheet display   79

Gridlines 80

Hiding columns 81

Showing columns..82

Fonts 83

Heights and widths..84

Freezing columns 85

Print Preview...86

Page Setup 88

Printing your table...89

Summary..90

8   Sorting and searching   91

Find..92

Filter by selection 93

Sort 94

Multi-level sorts 95

Saving queries..97

Multi-table queries 98

Setting the Query criteria 100

Reusing queries..102

Query Wizard..104

Summary..108

9 Forms   **109**

Designing a form 110

Headers and footers 112

Adding fields 115

Save your form 116

Form view 117

Using Form Wizard 118

Summary 124

10 Reports   **125**

The Report design screen 126

Grouping records 128

Sorting grouped records 130

Adding a text box 131

Preview and print 132

Mailing labels 133

Summary 138

Appendices   **139**

Database Wizard 140

A Accommodation table 144

B Contacts table 145

C Price table 146

Index   **147**

VIII

Preface

The computer is about as simple as a spacecraft, and who ever let an untrained spaceman loose? You pick up a manual that weighs more than your birth-weight, open it and find that its written in computerspeak. You see messages on the screen that look like code and the thing even makes noises. No wonder that you feel it's your lucky day if everything goes right. What do you do if everything goes wrong? Give up.

Training helps. Being able to type helps. Experience helps. This book helps, by providing training and assisting with experience. It can't help you if you always manage to hit the wrong keys, but it can tell you which are the right ones and what to do when you hit the wrong ones. After some time, even the dreaded manual will start to make sense, just because you know what the writers are wittering on about.

Computing is not black magic. You don't need luck or charms, just a bit of understanding. The problem is that the programs that are used nowadays look simple but aren't. Most of them are crammed with features you don't need – but how do you know what you don't need? This book shows you what is essential and guides you through it. You will know how to make an action work and why. The less essential bits can wait – and once you start to use a program with confidence you can tackle these bits for yourself.

The writers of this series have all been through it. We know your time is valuable, and you don't want to waste it. You don't buy books on computer subjects to read jokes or be told that you are a dummy. You want to find what you need and be shown how to achieve it. Here, at last, you can.

1 Getting started

What is a database? 2

Access objects 4

Preparing your data 6

Getting into Access 8

The Access screen 9

Summary 10

What is a database?

A **database** is simply a collection of data. It may be an address list, employee details or details of items in stock.

Access is a **relational** database - this means that all related data is stored in one place. If you are storing data about your business, you could have your employee data, customer data, product data, supplier data etc all stored in your Company Database.

Table

In a relational database, all the data on one topic is stored in a **table**. You would have a table for your employee data, a table for your customer data, a table for your product data etc. If your database requirements are fairly simple, you might have only one table in your database. If your requirements are more complex, your database may contain several tables.

The data in the table is structured in a way that will allow you to interrogate the data when and as required. All of the data on one item, eg an employee or a stock item, is held in the *record* for that employee or stock item, within the appropriate table.

Record

A **record** contains information about a single item in your table. All the detail relating to one employee will be held in that employee's record. All the detail on a customer will be held in a record for that customer. The detail is broken down into several *fields* – one for each piece of detail about your item (employee, stock item, etc).

Tip

If you have never used a database package before, I suggest you read through the next few pages carefully. Database concepts and jargon are not difficult, but you need to appreciate how a database works (in theory) and become familiar with some of the jargon you will come across. If you are already familiar with databases, move on to "Getting into Access".

COMPANY DATABASE FILE

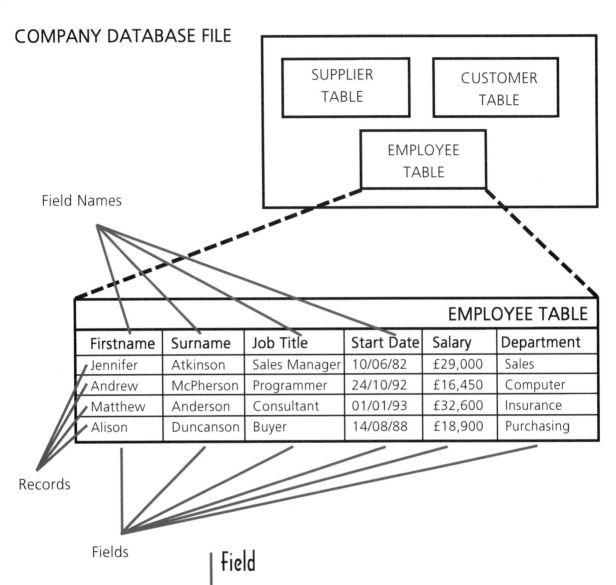

Field Names

Records

Fields

Field

A **field** is a piece of data within a record. In an employee's record things like firstname, surname, job title, address, age, salary etc would all be held in separate fields. In a stock item record, you would have fields for stock number, description, price etc.

Each field has a name that identifies it.

Access objects

When working in Access, you find six different types of **objects** that are used to input, display, interrogate, print and automate your work. These objects are listed in the Database Window.

Tables

Tables are the most important object in your database. Tables are used for data entry, viewing data and displaying the results of queries. (*See sections 3-8*)

In a Table each record is displayed as a **row** and each field is displayed as a **column**. You can display a number of records on the screen at any one time, and as many fields as will fit on your screen. Any records or fields not displayed can be scrolled into view as required.

Queries

You use **queries** to locate specific records within your tables. You might want to extract records that meet specific selection criteria (eg all employees on Grade G in the Accounts department). When you run a Query, the results are displayed in a Table. (*See section 8*)

Forms

You can use **forms** to provide an alternative to tables for data entry and viewing records. With forms, you arrange the fields as required on the screen - you can design your forms to look like the printed forms (invoices, order forms etc) that you use.

When you use forms, you display one record at a time on your screen. (*See section 9*)

Reports

Reports can be used to produce various printed outputs from data in your database.

Using reports, the same database can produce a list of customers in a certain area, a set of mailing labels for your letters, or a report on how much each customer owes you. (*See section 10*)

Macros & Modules

Macros and **modules** are used to automate the way you use Access, and can be used to build some very sophisticated applications.

They are well beyond the scope of a Made Simple book!

Rules for names

When setting up your database you need to name your Objects (Tables, Queries, Forms, Reports, Macros and Modules).

• Object names can be up to 64 characters in length

• They can include any characters *except:*

> a full stop (.)
> an exclamation mark (!)
> an accent grave (`) or
> brackets ([])

Tip

Learn to recognise these tabs — they can speed up your work.

Preparing your data

The most important (and often most difficult) stage in setting up your database takes place away from the computer. Before you set up a database you must get your data organised. You must ask yourself two key questions

● What information do I want to store?

● What do I want to get out of my database?

NB You must also work out your answers to these two questions!?!

Once you've decided what you are storing, and what use you intend to make of the data, you are ready to start designing your database. Again, much of this can be done away from the computer.

What fields do you need?

You must break the data down into the smallest units you will want to search or sort on. Each of these must be a separate field.

If you are setting up **names**, you would probably break the name into three fields - *Title, Forenames* (or initials) and *Surname.* This way you can sort the file into Surname order, or search for someone using the Forename and Surname.

If you are storing **addresses**, you would probably want separate fields for *Town/city, Region* and/or *Country.* You can then sort your records on any of these fields, or locate records by specifying appropriate search criteria. For example, using Town/city and Country fields, you could search for addresses in Perth (*Town/city*), Australia (*Country*) rather than Perth (*Town/city*), Scotland (*Country*).

Tip

When planning your database, take a small sample of the data to be stored and examine it carefully. Break each item into its smallest units (fields). You can then work out what fields you will need to be able to store all the necessary data for all the items.

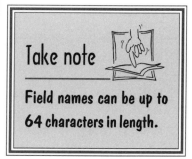

Take note

Field names can be up to 64 characters in length.

How big are the fields?

You must also decide how much space is required for each field. The space you allocate must be long enough to accommodate the longest item that might go there. How long is the longest surname you want to store? If in doubt, take a sample of some typical names (McDonald, Peterson, MacKenzie, Harvey-Jones?) and add a few more characters to the longest one to be sure. An error in field size isn't as serious as an error in record structure, as field sizes can be expanded without existing data being affected.

It is *very important* that you spend time organising and structuring your data *before* you start to computerise it – you will save yourself a lot of time and frustration in the long run!

Getting into Access

It is assumed that Access is already installed on your computer. If it isn't, you must install it (or get someone else to install it for you) before going any further.

If you are already working in Windows, save any files you want to keep, close down the application(s) you are working in and return to the Desktop.

If you are not working in Windows, switch on your computer (if necessary) and go into Windows.

You're now ready to start using Access.

1 Click the **Start** button

2 Point to **Programs** to open its menu

3 Click on **Microsoft Access**

4 Choose the way that you want to start work

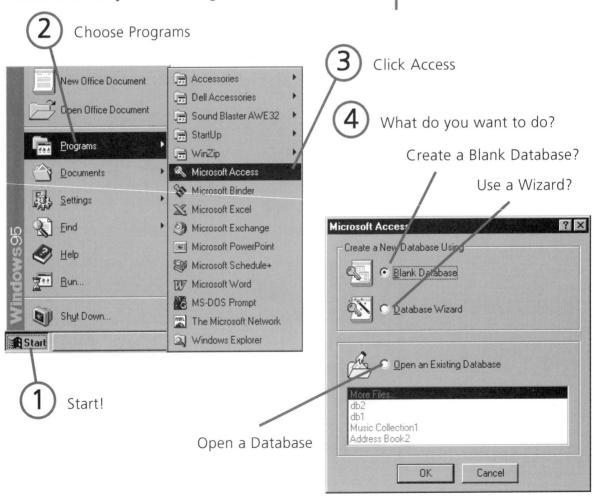

② Choose Programs

③ Click Access

④ What do you want to do?

Create a Blank Database?

Use a Wizard?

Open a Database

① Start!

8

The Access screen

Tip

If you need to know more about using the Windows 95 system, see "Windows 95 Made Simple".

Looking at the Access screen, you can identify the standard elements of any Window.

The Title Bar, Menu Bar and Toolbar; the Minimize, Maximize/Restore and Control Menu Buttons; and the Status Bar.

I suggest you Maximize the Access application window. This way you won't be distracted by other windows that may be open on your desktop.

Take note

When you've completed your session in Access, you must exit the package and return to the Windows environment — don't just switch off your computer. To exit Access, either click on the Close button, or open the File menu and select Exit.

Control Menu Button

Menu Bar

Title Bar

Toolbar

Minimize

Maximize/Restore

Close

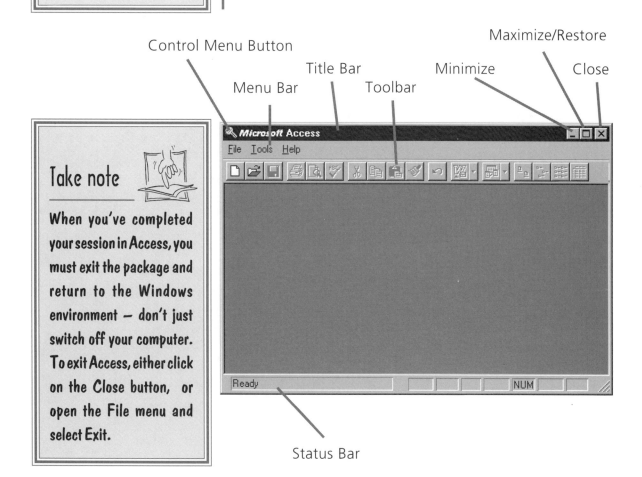

Status Bar

Summary

❏ A **database** is a collection of data

❏ Access is a **relational** database

❏ In a relational database, all related data is stored in one place

❏ A relational database is organised into **tables**, **records** and **fields**

❏ In Access, you will encounter various database objects - **tables**, **queries**, **forms**, **reports**, **macros** and **modules**

❏ **Preparation** is the first, very important, step in setting up your database

❏ To **get into Access**, click Start, Programs then Microsoft Access.

❏ To **get out of Access**, click the Close button on the Application window, or choose Exit from the File menu

2 Help

Contents tab 12

Instant Help 15

Index tab 16

Find tab 18

Answer Wizard 20

Summary 22

Contents tab

When working in the Windows environment there is always plenty of help available - in books, in manuals, in magazines and on-line. The trick is being able to find the help you need, when you need it. In this section, we look at the various ways you can interrogate the on-line Help when you discover you're in need of it.

The usual way into Help is through the Help Menu. We'll consider the Access Help Topics first. From the Help Topics dialog box, you can interrogate the Help system from the

- Contents tab
- Index tab
- Find tab
- Answer Wizard tab

We'll consider the Contents tab first. This is a handy place to "browse" to find out what's in the Help system.

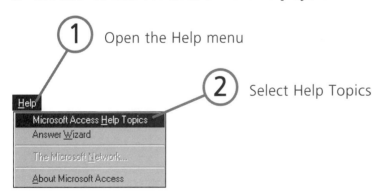

① Open the Help menu

② Select Help Topics

Basic Steps

1 Open the **Help** menu

2 Choose **Microsoft Access Help Topics**

3 At the **Help Topics** dialog box, select the **Contents** tab

4 Select a "book" that interests you

5 Click **Open** to open it

❏ With some topics you will be presented with more "books" to choose from

6 When you reach the topics, choose one

7 Click **Display**

8 Work through the system until you find the help you need

9 Close the Help system when you're finished

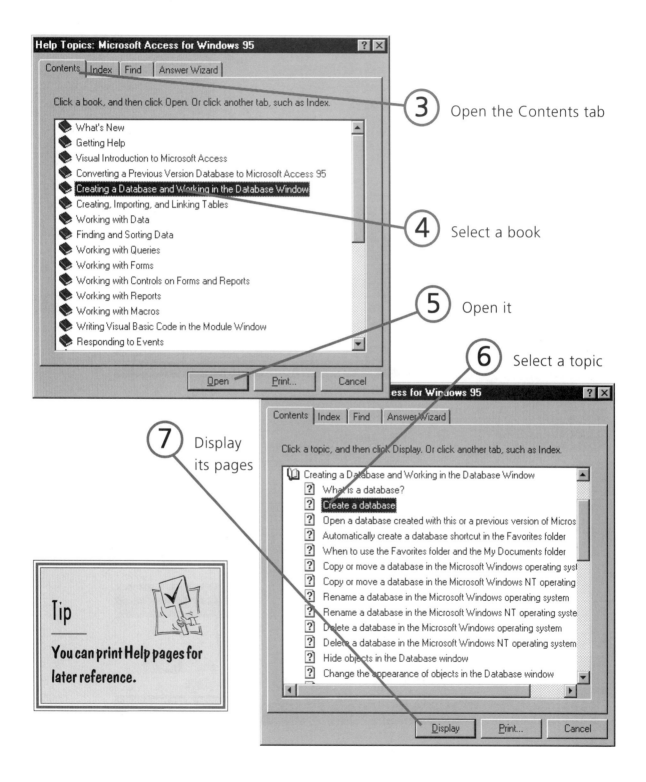

Help Topics: Microsoft Access for Windows 95

Contents | Index | Find | Answer Wizard

Click a book, and then click Open. Or click another tab, such as Index.

- What's New
- Getting Help
- Visual Introduction to Microsoft Access
- Converting a Previous Version Database to Microsoft Access 95
- Creating a Database and Working in the Database Window
- Creating, Importing, and Linking Tables
- Working with Data
- Finding and Sorting Data
- Working with Queries
- Working with Forms
- Working with Controls on Forms and Reports
- Working with Reports
- Working with Macros
- Writing Visual Basic Code in the Module Window
- Responding to Events

Open   Print...   Cancel

3 Open the Contents tab

4 Select a book

5 Open it

6 Select a topic

7 Display its pages

...ess for Windows 95

Contents | Index | Find | Answer Wizard

Click a topic, and then click Display. Or click another tab, such as Index.

- Creating a Database and Working in the Database Window
  - What is a database?
  - Create a database
  - Open a database created with this or a previous version of Micros
  - Automatically create a database shortcut in the Favorites folder
  - When to use the Favorites folder and the My Documents folder
  - Copy or move a database in the Microsoft Windows operating syst
  - Copy or move a database in the Microsoft Windows NT operating
  - Rename a database in the Microsoft Windows operating system
  - Rename a database in the Microsoft Windows NT operating syste
  - Delete a database in the Microsoft Windows operating system
  - Delete a database in the Microsoft Windows NT operating system
  - Hide objects in the Database window
  - Change the appearance of objects in the Database window

Display   Print...   Cancel

Tip

You can print Help pages for later reference.

13

Return to the Help Topics dialog box

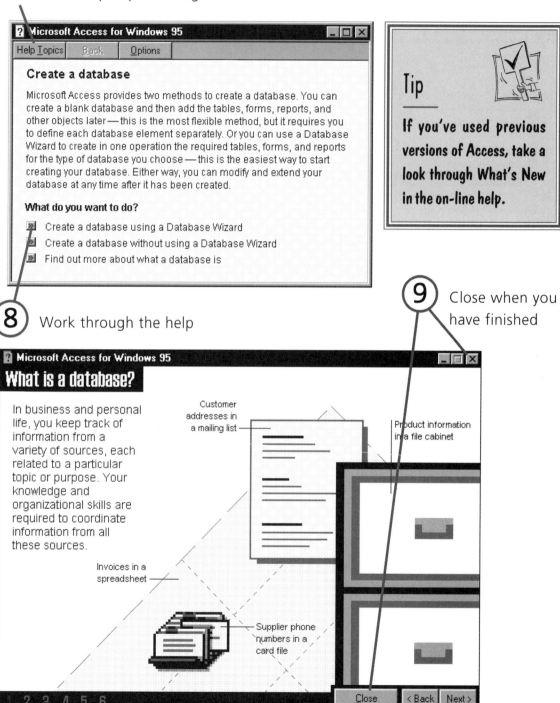

Microsoft Access for Windows 95

Help Topics | Back | Options

Create a database

Microsoft Access provides two methods to create a database. You can create a blank database and then add the tables, forms, reports, and other objects later — this is the most flexible method, but it requires you to define each database element separately. Or you can use a Database Wizard to create in one operation the required tables, forms, and reports for the type of database you choose — this is the easiest way to start creating your database. Either way, you can modify and extend your database at any time after it has been created.

What do you want to do?

» Create a database using a Database Wizard
» Create a database without using a Database Wizard
» Find out more about what a database is

Tip

If you've used previous versions of Access, take a look through What's New in the on-line help.

8 Work through the help

9 Close when you have finished

Microsoft Access for Windows 95

What is a database?

In business and personal life, you keep track of information from a variety of sources, each related to a particular topic or purpose. Your knowledge and organizational skills are required to coordinate information from all these sources.

Customer addresses in a mailing list

Product information in a file cabinet

Invoices in a spreadsheet

Supplier phone numbers in a card file

1 2 3 4 5 6   Close   < Back Next >

14

1 Click the Help tool on the Standard toolbar

2 Point and click on the tool or menu/menu item you are interested in

3 Click anywhere off the tool to close the description

Help tool

You can get help on any tool on a displayed toolbar, or on any menu item, using the Help tool. This will show you a panel giving a brief description of the function of the tool or menu item.

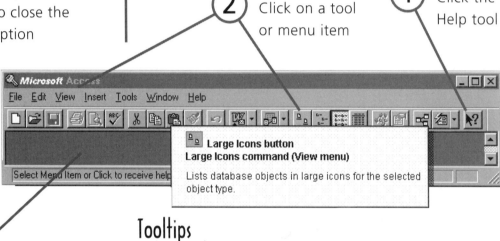

② Click on a tool or menu item

① Click the Help tool

③ Click off the item to close the panel

Tooltips

If you point to any tool on a displayed toolbar, a tooltip appears to describe the function of the tool. The status bar displays a short description of the tool's function.

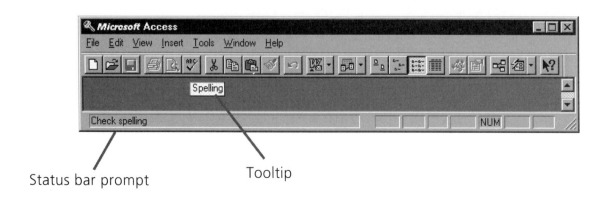

Status bar prompt

Tooltip

Index tab

As an alternative to the Contents tab, you can explore the Help system from the Index tab. This option gives you quick access to any topic and is particularly useful once you know what you are looking for!

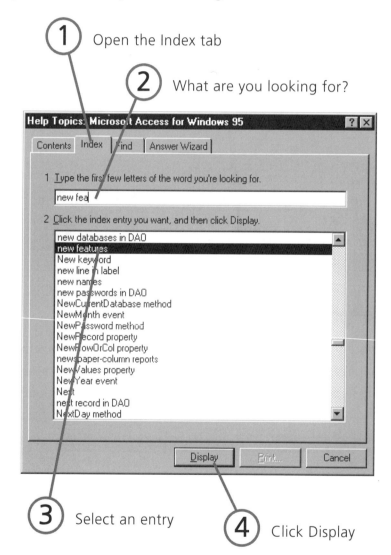

① Open the Index tab

② What are you looking for?

③ Select an entry

④ Click Display

Basic steps

1 At the **Help Topics** dialog box, select the **Index** tab

2 Start typing in the word you're looking for

3 When the index entry appears in the list, select it

4 Click **Display**

❑ A list of related topics will be displayed or the Help Text requested will appear (it depends on what you pick in the index)

5 Continue until you find the help you need

6 Close the Help window when you have finished

Related topics are
displayed

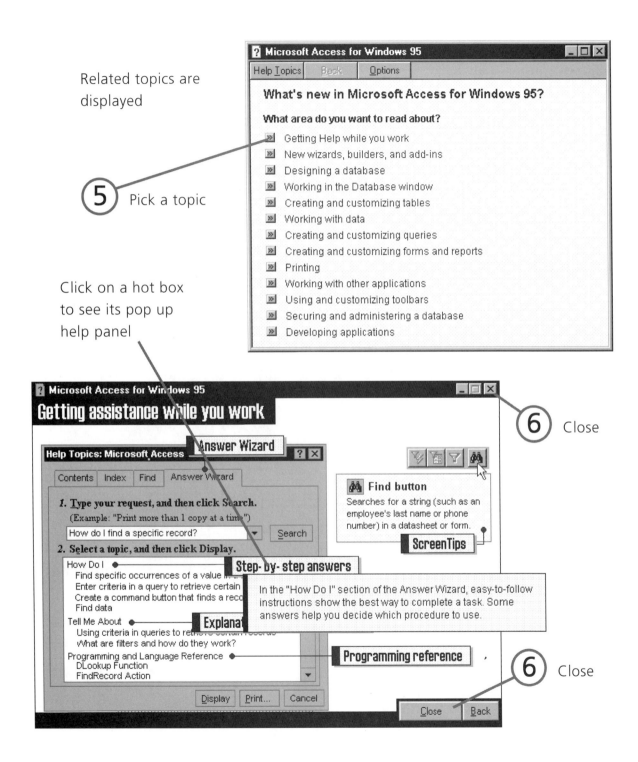

⑤ Pick a topic

Click on a hot box
to see its pop up
help panel

Microsoft Access for Windows 95

Help Topics | Back | Options

What's new in Microsoft Access for Windows 95?

What area do you want to read about?

» Getting Help while you work
» New wizards, builders, and add-ins
» Designing a database
» Working in the Database window
» Creating and customizing tables
» Working with data
» Creating and customizing queries
» Creating and customizing forms and reports
» Printing
» Working with other applications
» Using and customizing toolbars
» Securing and administering a database
» Developing applications

Microsoft Access for Windows 95

⑥ Close

Getting assistance while you work

Answer Wizard

Help Topics: Microsoft Access ? ×

Contents | Index | Find | Answer Wizard

Find button
Searches for a string (such as an
employee's last name or phone
number) in a datasheet or form.

ScreenTips

1. **Type your request, and then click Search.**
(Example: "Print more than 1 copy at a time")

How do I find a specific record? ▼ | Search

2. **Select a topic, and then click Display.**

How Do I
  Find specific occurrences of a value in
  Enter criteria in a query to retrieve certain
  Create a command button that finds a reco
  Find data
Tell Me About
  Using criteria in queries to ret
  What are filters and how do they work?
Programming and Language Reference
  DLookup Function
  FindRecord Action

Step-by-step answers

Explanat

In the "How Do I" section of the Answer Wizard, easy-to-follow
instructions show the best way to complete a task. Some
answers help you decide which procedure to use.

Programming reference

⑥ Close

Display | Print... | Cancel

Close | Back

17

Find tab

You can use the Find tab to search out specific words and phrases, rather than look for a particular category of information.

If this is the first time you've used the Find tab the Find Setup Wizard runs to set up your word list - just follow the prompts to set up your list (this only happens once).

The Minimize option should do all you need

Work through the Wizard

You will have a brief wait while the word list is created

Basic steps

1 Select the **Find** tab

2 Type in your word (or part of it - enough to get some matching words displayed)

3 Select a matching word to narrow the search

4 Choose a topic

5 Click **Display**

6 Close the Help when you are done

Take note

This option is not the easiest way to get help if you're new to Access. It can be difficult to find help on "simple" things!

① Open the Find tab

Help Topics: Microsoft Access for Windows 95   **? X**

Contents | Index | Find | Answer Wizard |

1 Type the word(s) you want to find

| delete | | ▼ | Clear

② Key in your text

2 Select some matching words to narrow your search   Options...

DeleteObject
DeleteQuerydef
DeleteQueryDef
DeleteReportControl
deletes
Deletes
DeleteSetting

Find Similar...

Find Now

Rebuild...

③ Narrow the search

3 Click a topic, then click Display

Create a command button that adds, deletes, duplicates, prints, saves, or und
Create, delete, or alter tables, or create indexes using an SQL data-definition c
Delete a control
Delete a field from a table in Datasheet view
Delete a field from a table in Design view
Delete a sorting or grouping field or expression in a report
Delete Method (DAO)

④ Pick a topic

| 45 Topics Found | | All words, Begin, Auto, Pause |

⑤ Click Display

Display | Print... | Cancel

? Microsoft Access for Windows 95   _ □ X

Help Topics | Back | Options |

⑥ Close

Delete a field from a table in Datasheet view

1 In table Datasheet view, click the field selector of the column you want to delete.

2 On the Edit menu, click Delete Column.

3 Microsoft Access asks if you want to continue.

   To delete the field and any data it contains, click Yes.

   To cancel the deletion, click No.

Caution You cannot undo the deletion of a field after clicking Yes. If you do click Yes, Microsoft Access permanently deletes both the field definition and the data it contains. To cancel the deletion, click No when Microsoft Access asks if you want to continue.

Notes

• If other database objects contain references to a deleted field, you need to delete those references as well. For example, if a report includes a control to print a field that has been deleted, Microsoft Access won't be able to find the data from the field and will generate an error message.

• You can't delete a field that's part of a relationship. You must delete the relationship first.

Answer Wizard

Using the Answer Wizard, you can interrogate the Help system by asking it questions in English. The phrasing of the questions improves with practice, but things like "How do I create a new table?" or "How do I print a report?" do work.

Basic steps

1 Select the **Answer Wizard** tab

2 Type in your question – the more practice you have at this, the better you get at phrasing your questions

3 Click **Search**

4 Choose a topic from the list

5 Click **Display**

6 Work through the Answer Wizard steps as prompted

❑ The Wizard may demonstrate the procedure, and display instructions

7 Close Help once you've found the help you need

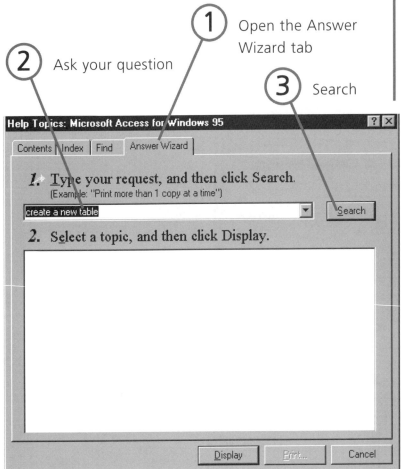

① Open the Answer Wizard tab

② Ask your question

③ Search

Help Topics: Microsoft Access for Windows 95

Contents | Index | Find | Answer Wizard

1. Type your request, and then click Search.
(Example: "Print more than 1 copy at a time")

`create a new table`

Search

2. Select a topic, and then click Display.

Display | Print... | Cancel

20

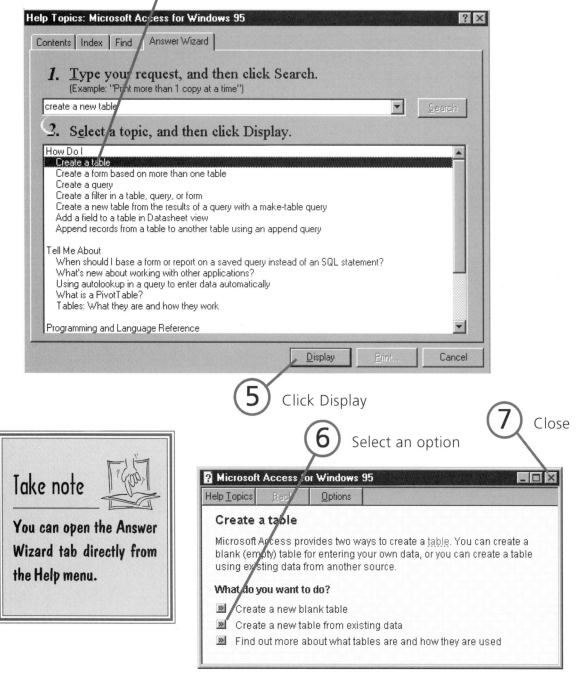

④ Choose a topic

Help Topics: Microsoft Access for Windows 95

Contents | Index | Find | Answer Wizard

1. Type your request, and then click Search.
(Example: "Print more than 1 copy at a time")

create a new table

Search

2. Select a topic, and then click Display.

How Do I
Create a table
Create a form based on more than one table
Create a query
Create a filter in a table, query, or form
Create a new table from the results of a query with a make-table query
Add a field to a table in Datasheet view
Append records from a table to another table using an append query

Tell Me About
When should I base a form or report on a saved query instead of an SQL statement?
What's new about working with other applications?
Using autolookup in a query to enter data automatically
What is a PivotTable?
Tables: What they are and how they work

Programming and Language Reference

Display | Print... | Cancel

⑤ Click Display

⑦ Close

⑥ Select an option

Take note

You can open the Answer
Wizard tab directly from
the Help menu.

Microsoft Access for Windows 95

Help Topics | Back | Options

Create a table

Microsoft Access provides two ways to create a table. You can create a
blank (empty) table for entering your own data, or you can create a table
using existing data from another source.

What do you want to do?

» Create a new blank table
» Create a new table from existing data
» Find out more about what tables are and how they are used

21

Summary

- ❑ To get into the Access Help system, select **Microsoft Access Help Topics** from the Help menu

- ❑ **Browse** through the Help from the Contents tab

- ❑ **Tooltips** and the **Help tool** are useful learning aids when you start out using Access

- ❑ **Search** for specific categories of information from the Index tab

- ❑ **Locate** help on specific words using the Find tab

- ❑ **Ask questions** of the Help system using the Answer Wizard

3 Building a database

Creating a new database 24

Creating a new table 26

Table design window 28

AutoNumber field 30

Date/Time fields 33

Text field 36

Yes/No field 38

Number field 40

Memo field 42

Primary key 43

Saving the design 44

Summary 46

Creating a new database

The first thing we have to do is create a database for our data, and give the database a suitable name.

Choose Blank Database

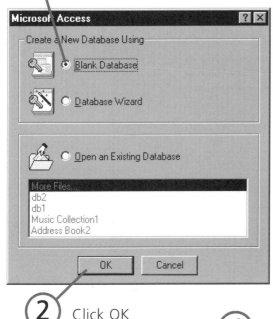

Click OK

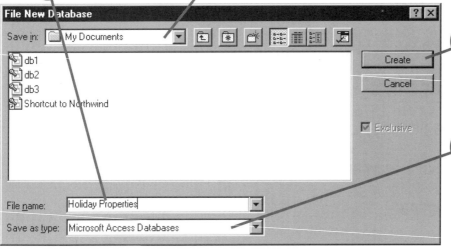

Type in a name

Select a folder

Click Create

Leave at the default

Basic steps

1 Choose **Blank Database** at the startup dialog

2 Click OK

or **From Within Access**

1 Open the **File** menu and choose **New Database** or click 🗋

2 Choose **Blank Database** from the **General Tab**

3 At the **File New Database**, enter a **File Name**. Here it is called *Holiday Properties*

4 Set the folder

5 Leave the **Save as type:** at *Microsoft Access Databases*

6 Click Create

The Project

In the next few sections, I've described a project that you could work through if you wish. Though it is somewhat limited, it will demonstrate many of the Access features you need to get to grips with.

You have set up a travel service that has an extensive database of quality accommodation.

Your clients will contact you with details of:-

● where they want to go

● when they want to go

● how many people need to be accommodated

● what kind of board eg self catering, is required

You can then interrogate your database to get a list of properties that match their requirements and check prices. If a client decides to make a booking, you can get the name, address and phone number of the property's owners, and contact them to arrange the let.

Your **HOLIDAY** Database will consist of 3 tables:

● **Accommodation** details

● **Price** details

● details of the property owner or **Contact**

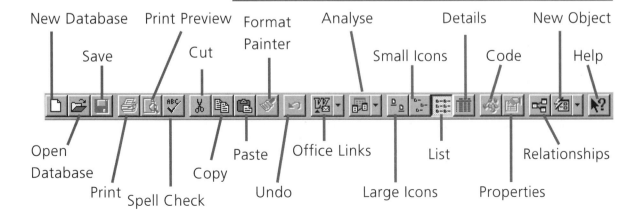

New Database · Save · Open Database · Print · Spell Check · Print Preview · Cut · Copy · Paste · Format Painter · Undo · Analyse · Office Links · Small Icons · Large Icons · List · Details · Code · Properties · New Object · Relationships · Help

Creating a new table

The data you store will be held in a table (or tables). The table consists of

● the record **structure**, that is the Field Names, Data Types and Descriptions

and

● the record **detail**, for example accommodation details, price details, personnel details

Give careful consideration to your table structure. It can be edited (you can add fields, delete fields and change the field properties) at a later stage, but things are a lot easier if you get it right to begin with.

You must decide:-

● what **fields** you require in your Table

● what kind of data will go in the field, e.g. text, date, number etc

● which field will be your **key field** - a field that uniquely identifies the record

Once you've worked out the structure, you can then create your table.

Basic steps

1 Ensure the **Tables Object Tab** is selected in your Database window

2 Choose **New**

3 At the **New Table** dialog box, choose **Design View**

4 Click **OK**

Tip

Good planning at the start is the secret of good databases. Be clear about what you want to store and what you intend to do with the data once it's stored.

Take note

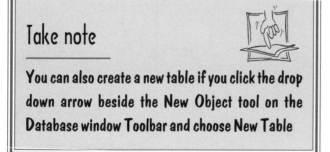

You can also create a new table if you click the drop down arrow beside the New Object tool on the Database window Toolbar and choose New Table

AutoForm
AutoReport
New Table
New Query
New Form
New Report
New Macro
New Module

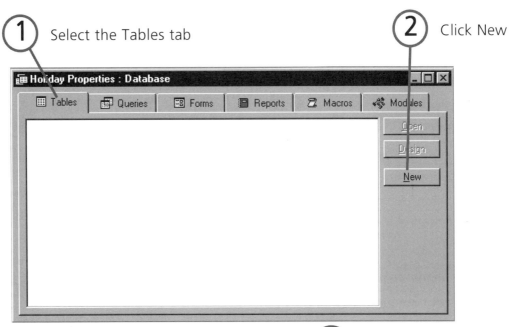

Take note

In your Database Window, the name of your database appears in the Title Bar, and the various objects that you can build into your database are listed on tabs along the top of the window.

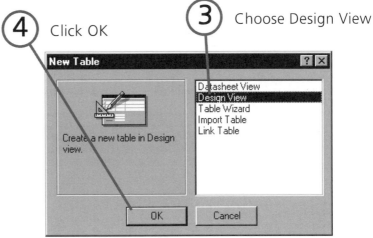

We will eventually set up three tables - the first one will hold details of the holiday accommodation we have on offer. There are different types - cottages (C), flats (F), apartments (A) and rooms (R) throughout Europe. Board is either self catering (SC), bed and breakfast (BB) or half board (HB). Properties may have a swimming pool, maid service or garden. Prices depend on the time of year.

Table design window

You will notice that the Table Design window has two panes - one that lets you specify the **Field Name**, **Data Type** and **Description**, and the other where you can specify the **Field Properties**.

You can use the **Field Properties** pane to customise the format of the field you are defining. The amount of customisation permitted depends on the Data Type selected for the field, for example

● the number of characters in a Text field

● the format in a Date/Time field

● the decimal accuracy of a Number field

● whether Duplicate entries are permitted in a field

We'll consider some of the field properties in the next few pages.

The table we are about to design is our Accommodation table. A summary of the fields and their properties is shown opposite. Full instructions will be given to help you set up the first field for each data type. You can then check the list to get details of the other fields of the same type.

Switch between the panes by pressing **[F6]**, or using the mouse.

Take note

Table Design has its own toolbar. Most of the tools will be introduced in the next few sections.

28

Accommodation Table

FIELD NAME	DATA TYPE	FORMAT/FIELD SIZE	OTHER FIELD PROPERTIES
Reference	AutoNumber	General	Primary Key. Indexed (No Duplicates)
Season Start	Date/Time	Short Date	Input Mask 99/99/00
Season End	Date/Time	Short Date	Input Mask 99/99/00
Country	Text	20	Indexed
Type of Accommodation	Text	1	Validation Rule ="C" or ="F" or ="A" or ="R"
Board	Text	2	Validation Rule ="SC" or ="BB" or ="HB"
Swimming Pool	Yes/No	Yes/No	
Maid Service	Yes/No	Yes/No	Default Value = Yes
Garden	Yes/No	Yes/No	
Price Range	Text	1	Description: Enter Code A-E Valid Rule ="A" or ="B" or ="C" or ="D" or ="E"
Sleeps	Number	Integer	Default Value = 4
ContactID	Number	Long Integer	Required = YES
Notes	Memo		

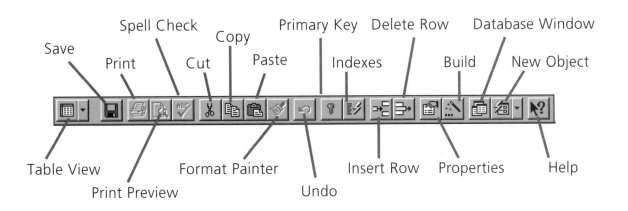

Save Spell Check Copy Primary Key Delete Row Database Window
Print Cut Paste Indexes Build New Object
Table View Format Painter Insert Row Properties Help
Print Preview Undo

AutoNumber field

Our first field will contain the accommodation code. This will be the unique identifier for each property – no two properties will have the same code. The field could be called something like Reference or Accommodation Code.

Fields that are used as identification fields in this way, can be completed automatically by Access. This is possible if the reference or identification field is given a AutoNumber data type. When you enter data into the finished table, Access automatically puts a 1 in the Reference field in the first record, 2 in the second record and so on. You *cannot* enter data into the field, and Access never uses the same number twice (even if records are added and deleted later), so the field is always unique.

Basic steps

1 Type in the first **Field Name** – names can be up to 64 characters long, including spaces.

2 Press **[Tab]**, or point and click, to move to the **Data Type** column

3 Click the down arrow for the **Data Types** list

4 Choose the type – **AutoNumber** this time

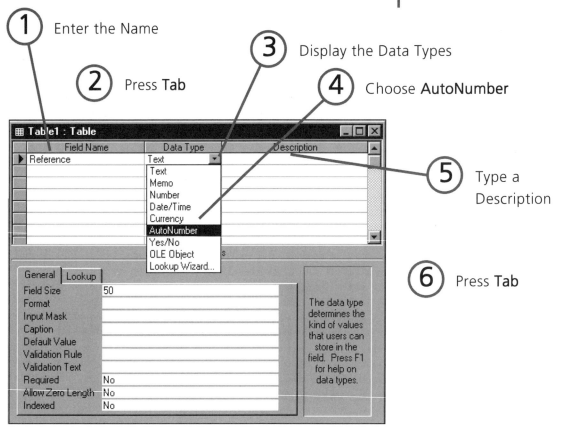

① Enter the Name

② Press **Tab**

③ Display the Data Types

④ Choose **AutoNumber**

⑤ Type a Description

⑥ Press **Tab**

Autonumber Fields Property Options

5 In the **Description** column, type in the message you want displayed on the Status Bar when you enter data to this field

6 Press **[Tab]** to move to the **Field Name** for your next field

With an AutoNumber Data Type, you can specify up to five Field Property options.

Field Size

Use the smallest practical field size setting because smaller data sizes are processed faster and require less memory. *Long Integer* is the smaller of the options available.

New Values

Leave this set at *Increment* to have the reference automatically incremented by 1 at each new record.

Format

You can specify the number format you want your AutoNumber field to adopt. If you drop down the list of pre-set formats, you can select the one that best suits your requirements.

If you prefer to specify your own format, simply key the number pattern (using permitted characters) in to the Format field. Characters that can be used include:-

0   to represent a Digit or 0

to represent a Digit or nothing

.   to represent the Decimal separator

" "   to represent a Literal (something that actually appears in the field)

Other permitted user characters are listed in the on-line help under Format Property.

The Format property option also appears in fields that have a Text data type.

Caption

In the Caption field, you can type in the label you want to appear beside the field when it is inserted into a **Form**. (We will deal with Forms later in the book.) A Caption can appear more "user-friendly" on a form than a field name does. If we use a field name like *Ref*, a suitable Caption for our field might be **Accommodation Code**.

This property option is present for all data types.

Indexed

Indexing fields can have the effect of speeding up searches (although the down side can be that updates are slower). If a field is designated the **Primary Key** (see page 43), this property is automatically set to *Yes, (No Duplicates)*.

This property option is present for all data types except Memo and OLE.

Take note

When specifying a Field's Properties, ensure that your insertion point is inside the correct Field in the upper pane, before you press [F6] to move to the lower pane. The current field is clearly indicated by the black arrow/triangle that appears in the selector column, to the left of the Field Name.

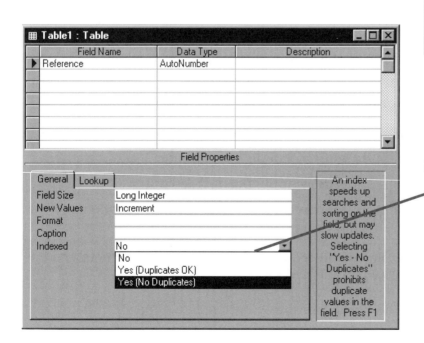

Indexed options

32

Basic steps

1 Type in *Season Start* in the **Field Name**

2 In the **Data Type** column select **Date/ Time** for this field

3 Press **[F6]** to switch to the **Field Properties** pane

4 Click the drop down arrow to display the list of **Format** options

5 Choose **Short Date**

6 Press **[F6]** to return to the upper pane

7 Key in a **Description** message if required (eg *"Only needed if not open all year"*)

8 Set up the *Season End* field in the same way.

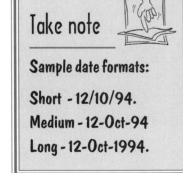

Take note

Sample date formats:

Short - 12/10/94.

Medium - 12-Oct-94

Long - 12-Oct-1994.

Date/Time fields

At our Season Start and Season End fields we are going to specify a Date/Time data type.

We will specify the format the date will take as DD/MM/YY (01/10/96 etc) – in other words we want what Access calls a Short Date format. This is specified in the Field Properties pane for the *Season Start* and *Season End* fields.

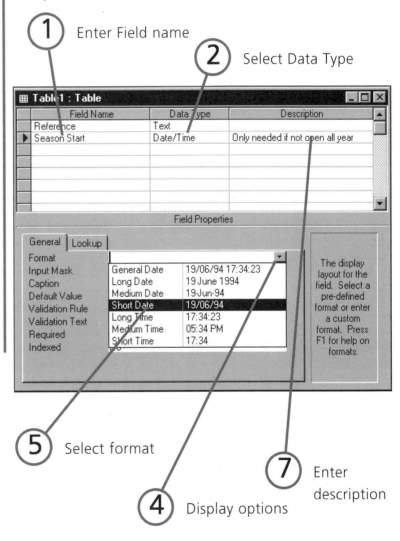

① Enter Field name

② Select Data Type

⑤ Select format

④ Display options

⑦ Enter description

Input mask

Regardless of how you choose to display your date, you will want to make sure that the date is keyed in accurately.

Different people might key in the same date with different separators between the day, month and year. 12/10/94, 12:10:94, 12-10-94 or 12.10.94 may all mean the 12th of October 1994 to us, but Access might not be so sure! To ensure that data entry is completed correctly, you can specify an **Input Mask**, or pattern, the data should take.

● The Input Mask does not affect the display Format.

Go back to the *Season Start* field to set up an Input Mask.

Basic steps

1 Position the insertion point in the *Season Start* field

2 Press [F6] to move to the lower pane

3 Move to the **Input Mask** field

4 Key in the pattern *99/99/00* (see Table opposite)

5 Press [F6] to move back to the upper pane

6 Do the same for the *Season End* field.

❑ When you do data entry to this field, an underscore will appear to indicate the position for each digit, and the slash character will be in place between the day, month and year sections (__/__/__) - it will not be necessary to key in the slash at data entry.

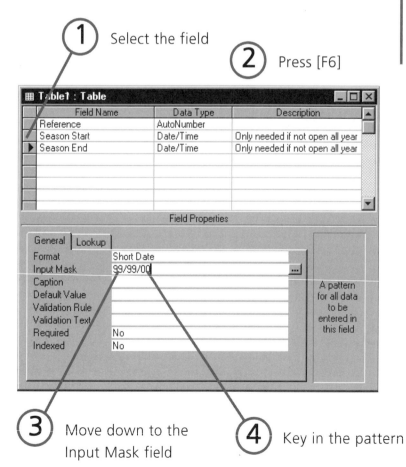

① Select the field

② Press [F6]

③ Move down to the Input Mask field

④ Key in the pattern

34

When setting up a pattern, you use special characters to show the type of input allowed, and whether or not input is *required*. These are listed here.

Character	Description
0	Digit (0-9). Plus (+) and Minus (-) signs not allowed. *Entry required.*
9	Digit or space. Plus and Minus signs not allowed.
#	Digit or space. Plus and Minus signs allowed.
L	Letter (A-Z). *Entry required.*
?	Letter (A-Z).
A	Letter or digit. *Entry required.*
a	Letter or digit.
&	Any character or a space. *Entry required.*
C	Any character or a space.
<	Convert all following characters to lower case.
>	Convert all following characters to upper case.
!	Causes input mask to fill from right to left when characters on the left side of the input mask are optional.
\	Causes the following character to be displayed as the literal character. ie \L is displayed as L, and doesn't mean 'Letter (A-Z)'. *Entry required*

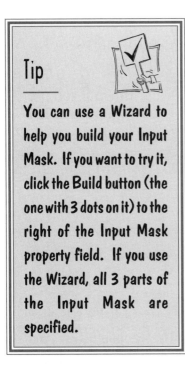

Tip

You can use a Wizard to help you build your Input Mask. If you want to try it, click the Build button (the one with 3 dots on it) to the right of the Input Mask property field. If you use the Wizard, all 3 parts of the Input Mask are specified.

An Input Mask can contain up to 3 parts, separated by semi-colon. ie *99/99/00;0;_*

The first part, *99/99/00*, specifies the Input Mask itself.

The second part specifies whether or not any literal display characters are stored with the data. *0* means that they are; *1* means that only the data is stored. The default is *0*.

The third part sets the character used to display spaces in the Input Mask. The default is the underline. If you want to use a space, enclose it in quotes ie *99/99/00;0; " "*

Text field

The next field in our Table is *Country*, which will hold the name of the country in which the holiday accommodation is located. This is a straightforward Text field, with a field size set to 20 (which should be long enough to store the countries we use).

1 Enter the **Field Name** ie *Country*

2 In the **Data Type** field, choose **Text**

3 Press **[F6]** to move to the lower pane

4 In the **Field Size**, key in the number of characters - 20 will do

5 Set the **Indexed** property option to *Yes (Duplicates OK)*

6 Press **[F6]** to return to upper pane

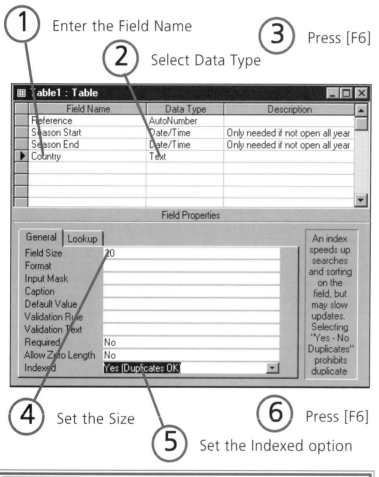

(1) Enter the Field Name

(2) Select Data Type

(3) Press [F6]

(4) Set the Size

(5) Set the Indexed option

(6) Press [F6]

An index speeds up searches and sorting on the field, but may slow updates. Selecting "Yes - No Duplicates" prohibits duplicate

Tip

Indexed fields are sorted faster than non-indexed ones , though data entry and update can be slower as a result.

Country, Type of Accommodation, Board and Price Range, may be sorted, and so should all be Indexed with duplicates allowed.

Take note

In Text fields the default size is 50 characters. The maximum is 255. If a size proves too small, it can be extended later.

Basic steps

1 Enter the **Field Name** - *Type of Accommodation*

2 Set the **Data Type** to **Text**.

3 Press **[F6]** to move down

4 Set the **Field Size**, to *1* - enough for our code

5 In the **Validation Rule**, key in *="C" or ="F" or ="A" or ="R"*

6 In the **Validation Text**, type a message to appear if the rule is not met. (Leave blank to get a standard error message).

7 Set the **Indexed** to *Yes (Duplicates OK)*

8 Press **[F6]** to go back to the upper pane

9 Key in a **Description** if required

❑ Set up the *Board* field, Size 2, and a Validation Rule on the code - *SC* for Self Catering, *BB* for Bed & Breakfast or *HB* for Half Board.

Validation Rule property option

The *Type of Accommodation* field is also a Text field. It can be a cottage, flat, apartment or room. We'll use a one character code for each type C, F, A or R. To avoid falling into the "rubbish in rubbish out" problem, we'll set a validation rule for this field, so that only the recognised codes can be entered.

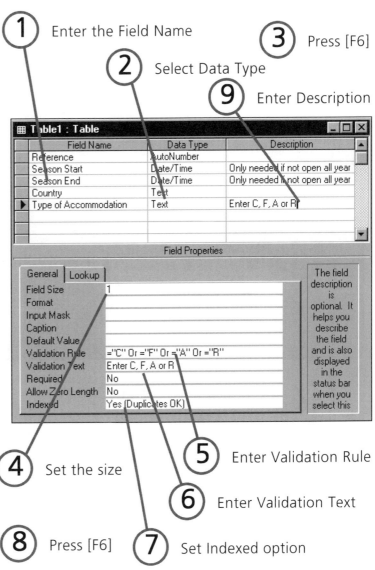

① Enter the Field Name

② Select Data Type

③ Press [F6]

⑨ Enter Description

④ Set the size

⑤ Enter Validation Rule

⑥ Enter Validation Text

⑦ Set Indexed option

⑧ Press [F6]

Yes/No field

If a field can have one of two values in it, eg *Yes* or *No*, *True* or *False*, *On* or *Off*, choose the **Yes/No** Data Type. The next three fields – Swimming Pool, Maid Service and Garden – are all Yes/No fields.

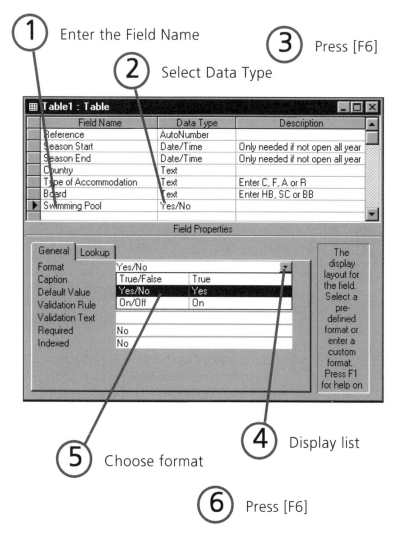

① Enter the Field Name

③ Press [F6]

② Select Data Type

⑤ Choose format

④ Display list

⑥ Press [F6]

Basic steps

1 Type in the **Field Name** - *Swimming Pool*

2 Set the **Data Type** to **Yes/No**

3 Press **[F6]** to move to the lower pane

4 Drop down the list of possible **formats**

5 Choose the one required

6 Press **[F6]** to return to the upper pane

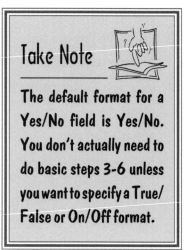

Take Note

The default format for a Yes/No field is Yes/No. You don't actually need to do basic steps 3-6 unless you want to specify a True/False or On/Off format.

Basic steps

Default value

1 Place the insertion point in the *Maid Service* field

2 Press **[F6]** to move to the lower pane

3 In the **Default Value**, type *Yes*

4 Press **[F6]** to move back to the upper pane

❑ Set up the *Garden* field in the same way as the *Swimming Pool* field.

The default value in a Yes/No field is *No*. As we know that most of our holiday accommodation has Maid Service, we can change the default value to *Yes* by typing *Yes* in the Default Value field of the lower pane for that field.

① Go to Maid Service

② Press [F6]

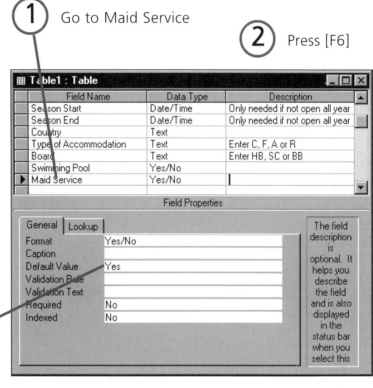

③ Key in Yes

④ Press [F6]

Take note

You will also have a 1 character Text field to set up for the Price Range field. This field could have a Validation Rule set to check that the appropriate range of codes are used -   ="A"   or ="B" or ="C" or ="D" or ="E"

Number field

In a Number field, you can specify the accuracy of the number that can be entered, by setting the Field Size property. In this example we have two number fields to set up - *Sleeps* and *ContactID*. With the *Sleeps* field, which holds how many people can be accommodated, the Field Size can be set to an **Integer** (you can't get 2.3 people!). With the *ContactID* field we must set the Field Size property to a **Long Integer**, as this field will eventually be used to set up a relationship between this table and the *Contacts* table.

As most of the holiday accommodation sleeps 4, we can set 4 as the Default Value for the field. On data entry, the field will be completed automatically, and it will only need editing when the number is something other than 4.

1 Key in the **Field Name** – *Sleeps*

2 Set the **Data Type** to **Number**

3 Press **[F6]** to move to the lower pane

4 Select **Integer** from the **Field Size** options

5 Place the insertion point in the **Default Value** and key in the value required, 4 in our case

6 Press **[F6]** to return to the upper pane

① Enter Field Name

② Set Data Type

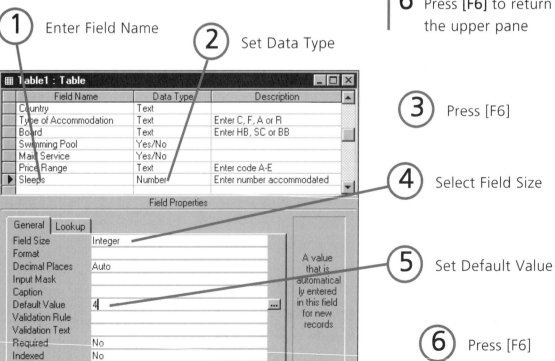

③ Press [F6]

④ Select Field Size

⑤ Set Default Value

⑥ Press [F6]

Basic steps

1 Key in the **Field Name** – *ContactID*

2 Set the **Data Type** to **Number**

3 Press **[F6]** to move to the lower pane

4 Set the **Field Size** to **Long Integer**

5 Set the **Required** property to **YES**

6 Press **[F6]** to return to the upper pane

Take note

On data entry, you will not be able to proceed to the next record until you have completed the ContactID field of the record you are entering.

Required property option

As the *ContactID* field will be used to link the *Accommodation* table with the *Contacts* table, we must have an entry in it. We will therefore set the **Required field** option to **Yes**.

(1) Enter Field Name   (2) Set Data Type

(3) Press [F6]

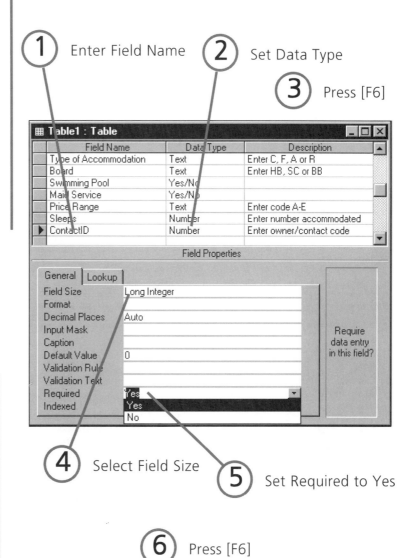

(4) Select Field Size   (5) Set Required to Yes

(6) Press [F6]

Memo field

Memo fields are used to add descriptive detail to your records. You can add "unstructured" notes in a Memo field. You can't sort or search on this field type, but it's very useful for holding all the additional things you feel are relevant. In our example, we can add details on the location of the accommodation, the places of interest nearby, the best food and wine to sample etc (anything we think our clients might want to know!).

Basic steps

1 Key in the **Field Name**
2 Set the **Data Type** to Memo
3 Type in a **Description** if required

① Enter Field Name
② Set Data Type
③ Enter Description

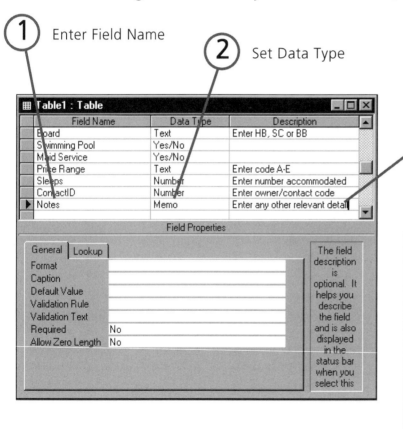

Take note

Memo fields can hold up to 64,000 characters, so they are very useful for lengthy text entries when you need to add comments or explanations. Memo fields cannot be indexed.

Basic steps

1 To select a single field to become your primary key, click the row selector at the left edge of the field.

2 Click the **Set Primary Key** tool 🔑

❑ Note the Key icon that appears to the left of the Key Field(s)

Primary key

Once you have completed specifying your table structure, and edited any fields you want to change, you should indicate which field is to be your **Primary key.** The Primary Key is a field (or combination of fields) that uniquely identifies each record in your table.

If you don't specify the Primary Key, Access can set one up for you the first time you save your design. It will set up a field called *ID* with an Autonumber data type if you do this.

We will specify the Reference field as our Primary Key.

The Key icon appears

① Click the row selector

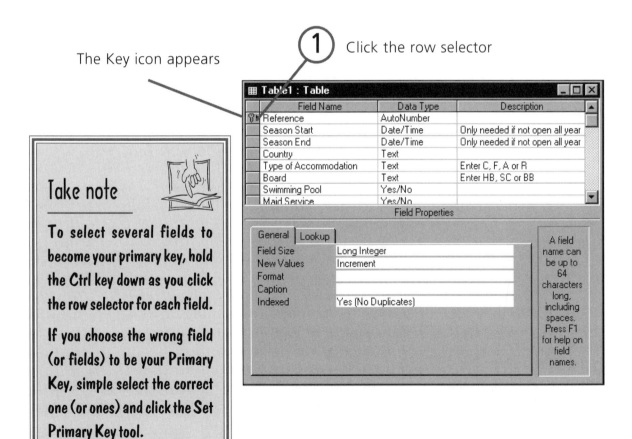

Take note

To select several fields to become your primary key, hold the Ctrl key down as you click the row selector for each field.

If you choose the wrong field (or fields) to be your Primary Key, simple select the correct one (or ones) and click the Set Primary Key tool.

Saving the design

Once you have your table design specified, you must **save** it. Once the design has been saved, you can decide whether you want to:-

● Leave data entry till later

or

● Move into the Datasheet View, so you can enter data straight away. (See Section 5 for data entry)

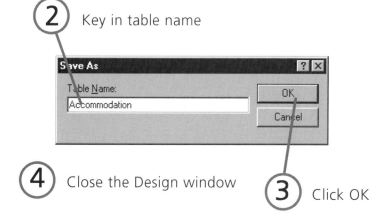

② Key in table name

④ Close the Design window

③ Click OK

Basic steps

❑ Save the Design for data entry later

1 Click the **Save** tool

2 At the **Save As** dialog box, type in *Accommodation* as the Table Name

3 Click **OK**

4 Close the Design window by clicking its **Close** button

❑ You will be returned to the Database window, with your new table listed on the Tables tab.

Take note

You can't exit the Design view without being reminded to save your Design if you haven't done so. If you don't want to save, choose NO at the *Must save changes first*, or *Save changes?* prompts, that appear.

Take note

After it has been saved once, and given a name, you only have to click on the Save icon to save any changes onto disk.

Basic steps

❑ **Save and move into the Datasheet view**

1 Click the **Save** tool

2 If the table has not been saved before, the **Save As** dialog box will open.

3 Click the **Datasheet View** tool

or

Click the down arrow beside the View tool

 and

choose **Datasheet View**

4 You arrive in Datasheet view ready for data entry.

Moving straight into into Datasheet view makes sense when you are ready to start work in earnest. For now, I suggest you close the Datasheet and leave data entry until you have got to Section 5.

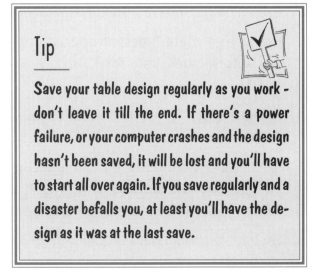

Tip

Save your table design regularly as you work - don't leave it till the end. If there's a power failure, or your computer crashes and the design hasn't been saved, it will be lost and you'll have to start all over again. If you save regularly and a disaster befalls you, at least you'll have the design as it was at the last save.

Note your new table in the Tables list

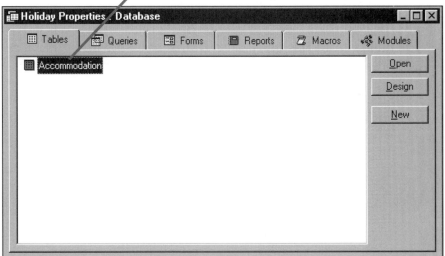

Summary

- To create a **new Database,** click the New Database tool on the toolbar

- To create a **new Table**, select the Tables tab on the Database window and click New

- Each field *must* have a **Field Name** and a **Data Type**

- Examples of **Data Types** introduced in this section are AutoNumber, Date/Time, Text, Yes/No, Number and Memo

- For each Data Type, you can set various **Field Properties** as required

- Field Properties introduced in this section included Format, Caption, Indexed, Input Mask, Validation Rule, Validation Text, Default Value and Required

- Each table should have a unique field (or fields) set as the **Primary Key**

- You should **save your table** design regularly as you build it up (using the Save tool on the toolbar)

- To **close your Table design** and return to the Database Window, click the close button

- To change from **Design** view to **Datasheet** view in your Table, click the Datasheet tool on the toolbar

4 Relationships

Adding a new table 48

Relationships 49

Making the relationship 50

Table Wizard 52

Checking relationships 56

Closing a database 59

Summary 60

Adding a new table

We now need to set up the other tables in our database. The next one is the *Price* table. Its fields, data types and other characteristics are shown here.

Create a new table, as shown on page 26, then move to the Table Design window and define the first field.

Field Name   Price Range

Data Type   Text, **Field Size** of 1 and add the **Validation Rule** ="A" or ="B" or="C" or ="D" or ="E"

Make this field the Primary Key. (See page 43)

All the other fields have the Currency data type.

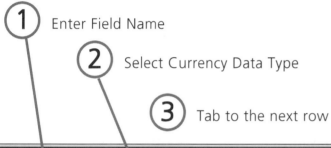

① Enter Field Name

② Select Currency Data Type

③ Tab to the next row

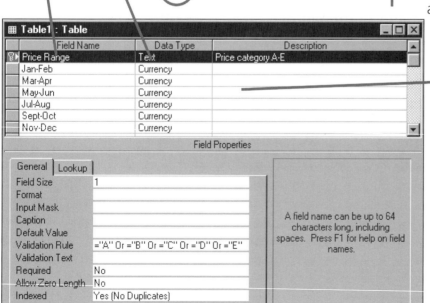

④ Complete the other rows

Basic steps

1 Key in the **Field Name** - *Jan-Feb*

2 Set the **Data Type** to **Currency**

3 [Tab] to the next row

4 Set up the remaining fields in this way, naming them – *Mar-Apr, May-Jun, Jul-Aug, Sept-Oct, Nov-Dec*

5 **Save** the Table Design

6 Return to the Database window to set the **Relationship** between the *Accommodation* and the *Price* table.

Basic steps

1 From the Database window, click the **Relationship** tool

or

1 Choose **Relationships..** from the **Edit** menu

❑ The **Relationships** and **Show Table** dialog boxes open. If the **Show Table** dialog box doesn't open, click the **Show Table** tool

2 Pick the *Accommodation* table from the list

3 Click [Add] to add it to the Relationships window. Add the *Price* table in the same way.

4 Click [Close] on the **Show Table** window.

Relationships

Once the table designs have been specified, it is time to indicate the relationships between the tables. Defining the relationships makes it easier to work with queries, forms and reports later on.

At this stage we want to set the relationship between the *Accommodation* and the *Price* tables. They are related through the *Price Range* field that appears in both tables.

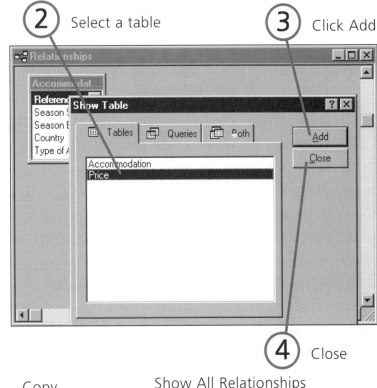

The Relationship toolbar

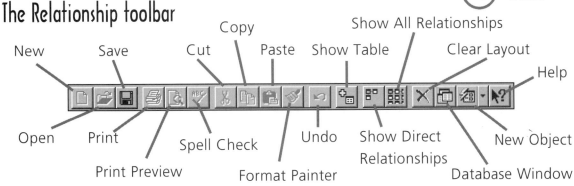

Making the relationship

We must now indicate how the two tables are related. The simplest type joins a field in each table, where the same values are held in each field. A relationship will normally be between the Primary key field in one table, and a similar field in another table. In our example the Primary key of the *Price* table is related to the *Price Range* field in the *Accommodation* table.

① Display the fields   **②** Drag and drop one onto the other

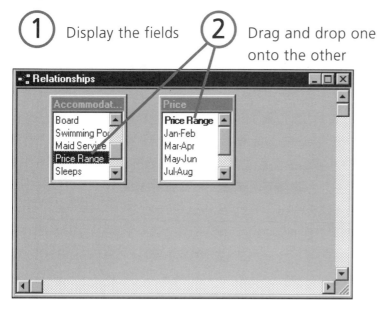

⑥ Create the join

③ Display and edit the relationship

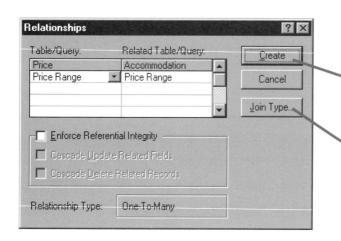

1 In the **Relationships** window, scroll through the list for each table until you can see the fields to be related – the *Price Range* fields

2 Drag and drop the field name from one table onto the related field in the other table

3 At the **Relationships** dialog box, if you want to edit the type of relationship, click
[Join Type...]

4 At the **Join Properties** dialog box, choose the type of join required – in our case, the first

5 Click [OK] to return to the **Relationships** window, with your selection set

6 At the **Relationships** dialog box, click [Create] to set the relationship

Now in the **Relationships** window, a line shows the related fields in your tables

7 Save the relationship with the **Save** icon 🖫

8 Close the **Relationships** window

❑ You are returned to the Database window.

❑ **To delete a relationship**

1 Click on the join line

2 Press the **[Delete]** key, and click [Yes] to confirm the Deletion.

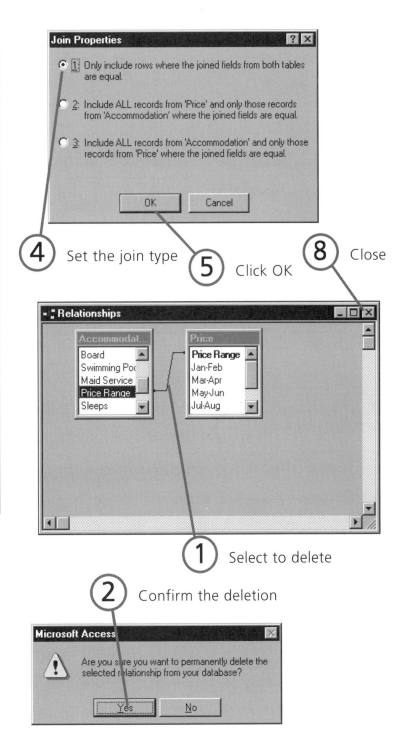

④ Set the join type

⑤ Click OK

⑧ Close

① Select to delete

② Confirm the deletion

Table Wizard

Instead of specifying your table design from scratch, you might find Table Wizard useful for some tables. We'll use it to set up our *Contacts* table for the Holiday database.

Basic steps

1 Click **New** on the Table tab at the Holiday database window

2 Choose **Table Wizard**

3 Click [OK]

4 In the **Table Wizard**, select the type of table – in our case **Business**

5 Choose *Contacts* from the **Sample Tables** list

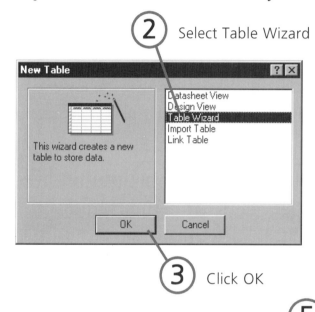

② Select Table Wizard

③ Click OK

④ Select category

⑤ Choose sample table

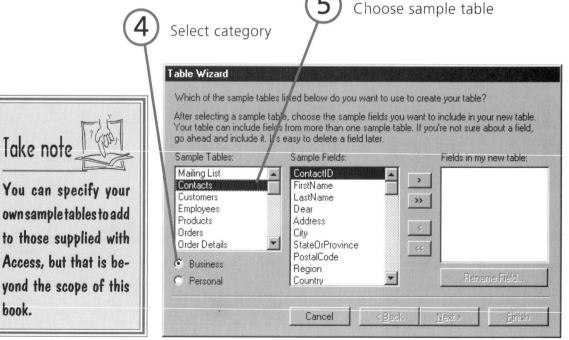

Take note

You can specify your own sample tables to add to those supplied with Access, but that is beyond the scope of this book.

Basic steps

Specifying the Fields

1 Select the **Field** you want to add to your own table from the **Sample Fields** list

2 Click the **Add** field button `>`

3 The field is added to the **Fields in my new table** list

4 Continue until you've added all the fields you need, then click `Next >` to move on to the next step

Using the table overleaf as a guide, select the fields you want to use in your *Contacts* table.

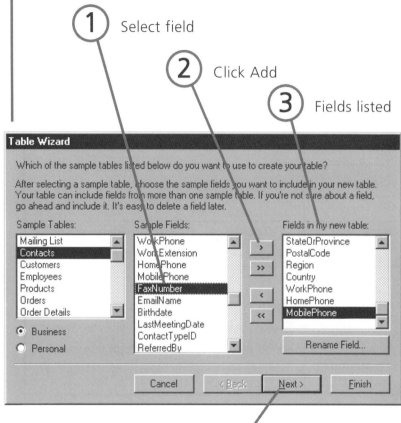

① Select field

② Click Add

③ Fields listed

④ Go to next step

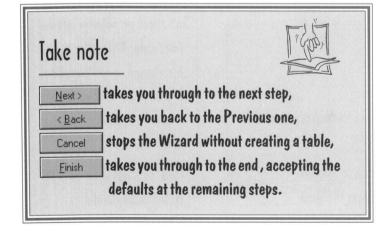

Take note

`Next >`	**takes you through to the next step,**
`< Back`	**takes you back to the Previous one,**
`Cancel`	**stops the Wizard without creating a table,**
`Finish`	**takes you through to the end, accepting the defaults at the remaining steps.**

Table Design

I suggest the following fields for your table. They hold the details of our property owners/contacts.

Contacts Table	
FIELD NAME	**NOTES**
ContactID	Primary Key- set this **after** fields are set up
First name	Set up using a Table Wizard therefore field attributes picked up from Wizard
Last Name	
Address	
City	
State	This field name is changed to *County* during set up process, or once the design is complete
Postal Code	
Workphone	Check field properties once design complete. Things like **Input masks** will need to be edited as they follow American conventions
Homephone	

New field names

❑ When adding fields to the list, the field name can be changed (e.g. State to County).

1 Add the field

2 Select it in the **Fields in my new table** list

3 Click [Rename Field...]

4 Key in the new name or edit the existing name

5 Click [OK]

6 Select the next field from the sample list.

Take Note

If you add a field by mistake, select it in the **Fields in my new table** list, and click the **Remove** field button [<]

The [>>] button adds all the sample fields to the list, the [<<] button removes all the fields from the list.

Basic steps

Finishing off

1 Edit the table name if necessary

2 Specify whether Access is to set the primary key (the default option) or you set it yourself

❑ I suggest you leave it at the default, this way the *ContactID* field is set as the Primary key, with an AutoNumber Data Type.

3 Click [Next >]

Once you have specified the field names for your table, the next step is to name the table and set the Primary Key.

Continue to work through the Table Wizard steps making any changes necessary.

(**1**) Enter table name

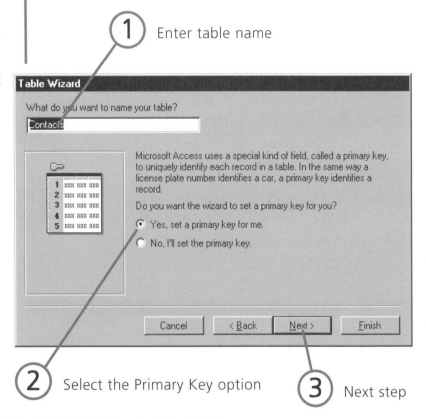

(**2**) Select the Primary Key option

(**3**) Next step

Take note

The ContactID fields in the Contacts and the Accommodation table will be the fields through which the Contacts and Accommodation tables are related. You can make this relationship at the end.

Checking relationships

Normally, if a database contains more than one table, each table is related to at least one other. In our *Accommodation* table there is a *ContactID* field, which holds the code of the contact. In the *Contacts* table, there is also a *ContactID* field (set as the Primary Key) that will hold the same codes. The two are therefore "related" through this common field.

The *Contacts* table is not related to the *Price* table.

Table Wizard displays a list of the tables in your database, and indicates whether or not they are related. (In some cases the Wizard makes the relationship between tables automatically).

You must check the relationships, and edit if necessary. In this example, you will need to set the relationship between the Accommodation and Contacts tables.

Basic steps

1 Select the table you want to check or change the relationship to

2 Click [Relationships...]

3 The current type of relationship is shown in the **Relationships** dialog box. If necessary, select an alternative option from the list

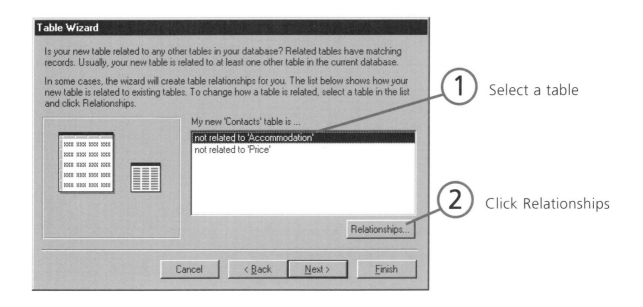

Select a table

Click Relationships

❏ In our case, the selected option, "One matches many", is correct. One Contact or owner may have several holiday properties (flats, cottages, apartments, rooms) in our Accommodation table.

4 Click **Cancel** if you want to exit without changing the settings. Click **OK** if you've changed a setting.

5 Once you are satisfied that the relationships are okay, click
Next > .

The new relationship between the tables is displayed.

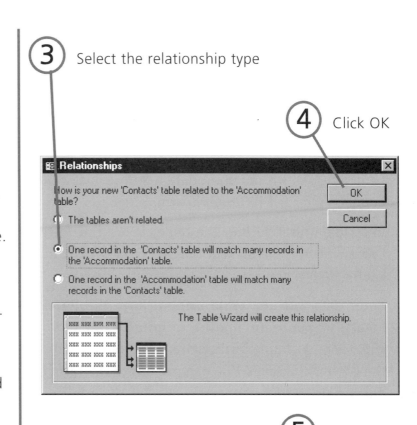

③ Select the relationship type

④ Click OK

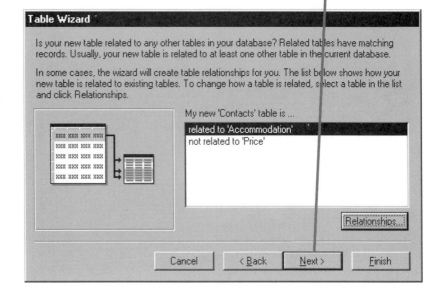

⑤ Click Next

Leaving Table Wizard

The last step is to choose where to go next.

- **Modify the Table Design** takes you to the Design screen, where you can make further modifications to the structure of your table. We need to do this. *Postal Code*, *WorkPhone* and *HomePhone* fields all have input masks that follow an American format. These should be deleted, so we can input data in our format. *State* could be changed to *County* at this stage too.

- **Enter data directly into the table** takes you to the Datasheet view. In this view, each record is a row, and each field is a column. This is the default option.

- **Enter data into the table using a form the Wizard creates for me**. If you choose this option, Table Wizard will design a simple form, that shows one record on the screen at a time. You can use either the form or datasheet to input, edit and view your records.

Basic steps

1 Select **Modify the Table** Design

2 Click [Finish]

3 At the **Table Design** window select a field

4 Press **[F6]** to move to the lower pane

5 Delete the entry in the **Input Mask** slot

6 Repeat for all fields as needed, then close the Table Design window

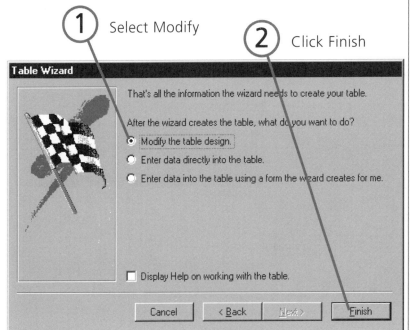

① Select Modify

② Click Finish

Take note

If you click [Finish] **once you have added all the fields (instead of** [Next >] **to go through each step), the wizard will give the table a default name and set the** *ContactID* **field as the Primary key (with a** *AutoNumber* **type). It will also take you straight into Datasheet view.**

Basic steps

1 Click the Close button on the Database window

❑ Your database is closed, but you are still in Access.

If you've finished working on your database, you might want to close it. You can close a database without leaving Access. If you exit Access, any open databases are closed as part of the exit routine.

1 Click to close

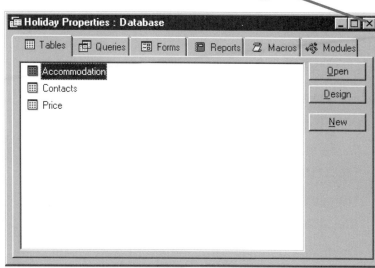

3 Select a field

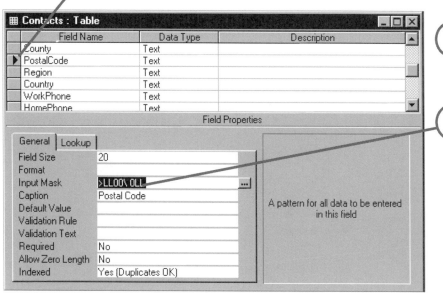

4 Press [F6]

5 Delete the Input Mask

Summary

❑ The **Currency** data type should be used for fields holding monetary values

❑ Most tables within your database will be **related** to at least one other table

❑ A relationship normally exists between the **primary key** field in one table and a similar field in another

❑ Click the **Relationships tool** to open the Relationships window

❑ To **make a relationship**, drag a field from one table, and drop it onto the related field in another

❑ To **delete a relationship**, select the join line and press **[Delete]** on your keyboard

❑ There are several **Table Wizards** to help automate the table design process

❑ To **close a database**, but remain in Access, click the close button on the Database window.

5 Data entry and edit

Opening a database 62

Opening a table 63

Using Datasheet view 64

Adding/deleting records 66

Using Form view 68

Summary 70

Opening a database

If the database you want to work on exists, but is not open, you must open it before you can work on it.

If you closed your database at the end of the last section, open it now so you can explore data entry in this section.

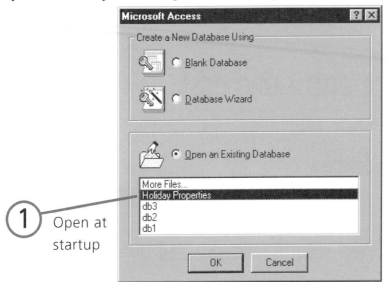

① Open at startup

1 Choose the database from the startup dialog

or **From within Access**

1 Click the **Open Database** tool 🗁

or

Choose **Open Database** on the **File** menu

2 At the **Open Database** dialog box, select the database to open

3 Double click the name or click ⌷ Open ⌷

---

① Choose File – Open Database..

② Select

③ Click Open

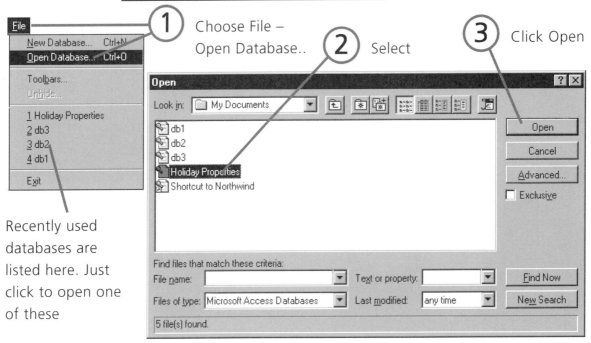

Recently used databases are listed here. Just click to open one of these

Basic steps

❏ To open a table in Datasheet view

1 Select the **Tables** tab in the **Database** window if necessary

2 Highlight the table you want to open

3 Double click on the name or click

   Open

Take note

If you have been working in Design view on a table, you can go directly to Datasheet view by clicking the Datasheet icon on the toolbar.

Opening a table

Once you have set up the structure of your table, the next stage is data entry. The table must be open for this, and it should be displayed in **Datasheet** view (rather than Design view). In this view, each column of the table is a field and each row is a record. We will start by looking at the *Accommodation* table.

1 Check the Tables tab is open

2 Select a table   **3** Click Open

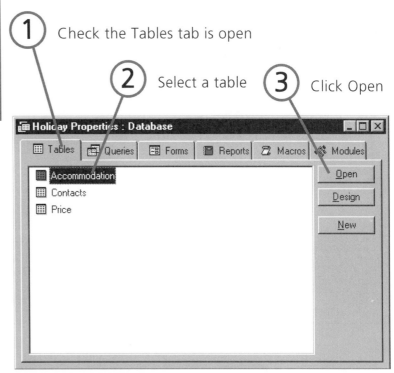

Tip

To open a table in Design view, select the table required and click   Design   .

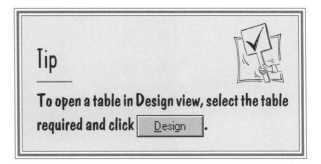

63

Using Datasheet view

Move from field to field in your table using:

[Tab]   to take you forward to the next field

[Shift]-[Tab]   to take your back to the previous field

Each record is saved when you move onto the next.

●   If you are using the project example, there is sample data for all three tables in Appendix A.

Take note

When entering data, if you find an error has been made at the Design stage, you can go into Design view by clicking ▣ ▾ .

Record being written

Incremented automatically

Input Mask

Default No

Default Yes

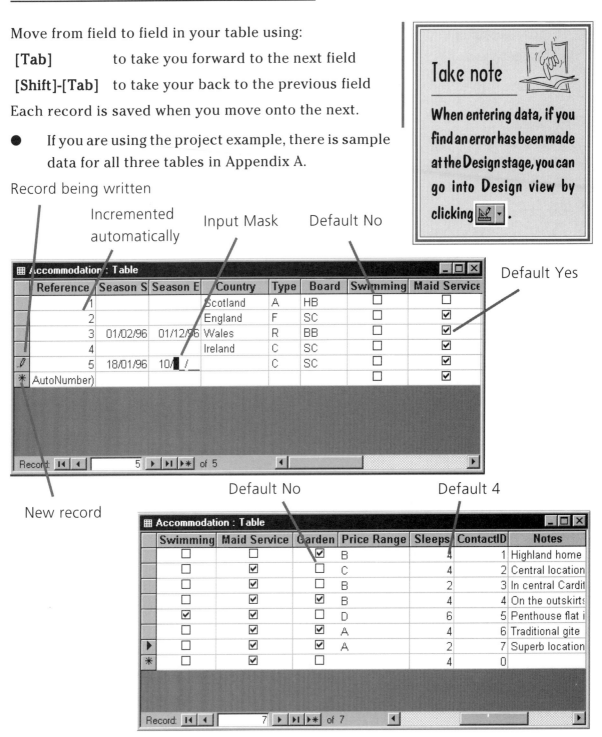

New record

Default No

Default 4

Editing

❑ You can edit data at any time. If you move onto a field using [Tab] or [Shift]-[Tab], the data in that field is selected.

You can then:

Replace the current contents, by just typing new data while the old is highlighted

Edit the data – press [F2] to deselect the text, then position the insertion point within the field using the [Arrow] keys

Erase the contents, by pressing [Delete].

Inappropriate entries

If you enter incompatible data for the Data Type specified in a field (ie if you put text in a number field, or try to key something in that disagrees with the Input Mask for that field), Access will display an error message. This will either be a standard error message, or one you keyed in to the Validation Text field at the design stage.

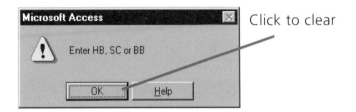

Click to clear

Moving around your datasheet

In addition to **[Tab]** and **[Shift]–[Tab]** to move between fields, there are other ways to move around.

● Point and click with the mouse to go to any field (using the vertical and/or horizontal scroll bars as necessary to bring the field into view).

● Use the arrows to the left of the horizontal scroll bar.

● To go to a specific record, press **[F5]**, key in the record number and press **[Enter]**.

And see the Keyboard Shortcuts, overleaf.

Go to first record   Next record

Previous record   Go to last record

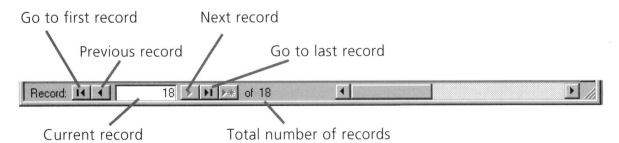

Current record   Total number of records

Adding/deleting records

Basic steps

Adding new records

When adding new records to your table, you add them to the **end** of the list of existing records. If you do not really want them at the end of the list, you will soon find out that it is very easy to sort the records into the order you want (rather than leaving them in input order)

1 Click the **New Record** tool ▶* or ▶* button

2 You are moved to the first field of the first empty row under the existing records

3 Enter the new record(s)

4 Close the datasheet or continue editing as required

2 A new row is created at the end

	Reference	Season S	Season E	Country	Type	Board	Swimming
	9			France	C	SC	☐
	10			Scotland	A	HB	☑
	11			England	F	SC	☑
	12			Wales	A	BB	☑
	13			Scotland	F	SC	☐
	14			Italy	C	SC	☑
	15			Spain	A	SC	☑
	16			England	C	SC	☐
	17			Orkney	C	SC	☐
	18			Jersey	A	SC	☑
	19			Ireland	R	HB	☑
	20			France	R	BB	☐
▶	(AutoNum)						☐

⊞ Accommodation : Table

Record: ◄◄ ◄ 21 ► ►◄ ►* of 21

3 Key in records

Keyboard shortcuts

[PageUp]	Moves you up a page	[Up arrow]	Current field, previous record
[PageDown]	Moves you down a page	[Down arrow]	Current field, next record
[Ctrl]-[PageUp]	Moves you left a page	[Ctrl]-[Up arrow]	Current field, first record
[Ctrl]-[PageDown]	Moves you right a page	[Ctrl]-[Down arrow]	Current field, last record
[Home]	First field, current record	[Ctrl]-[Home]	First field, first record
[End]	Last field, current record	[Ctrl]-[End]	Last field, last record

Deleting records

When some of your records become redundant, you will want to delete them. Be careful when deleting records - make sure you are really finished with them first!

Take note

To select several adjacent records, click and drag in the row selector area until you have highlighted all the records you want to delete.

(1) Select the record

	Reference	Season S	Season E	Country	Type	Board	Swimming	Maid
	8			Germany	C	SC	☐	
	9			France	C	SC	☐	
	10			Scotland	A	HB	☑	
▶	11			England	F	SC	☑	
	12			Wales	A	BB	☑	
	13			Scotland	F	SC	☐	
	14			Italy	C	SC	☑	
	15			Spain	A	SC	☑	
	16			England	C	SC	☐	
	17			Orkney	C	SC	☐	
	18			Jersey	A	SC	☑	
	19			Ireland	R	HB	☑	
	20			France	R	BB	☐	
*	AutoNumber)						☐	

Record: I◀ ◀ [11] ▶ ▶I ▶* of 20

(3) Confirm the deletion

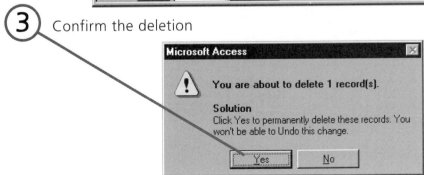

Microsoft Access

⚠ You are about to delete 1 record(s).

Solution
Click Yes to permanently delete these records. You won't be able to Undo this change.

[Yes] [No]

Using Form view

If you don't like working in Datasheet view, or would prefer to see one record at a time displayed in a simple form layout rather than several records at a time in rows, try using a Form. We will look at designing forms later, but you can let Access create a simple form for you using **Autoform**. This will take the fields, and list them in a basic form, with the table name shown at the top of each record.

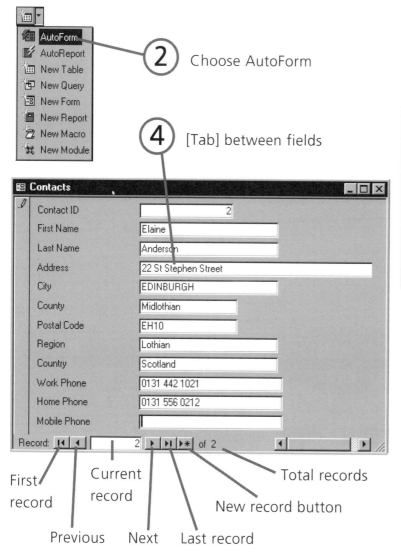

② Choose AutoForm

④ [Tab] between fields

First record
Current record
Previous
Next
Last record
New record button
Total records

Basic steps

1 At the **Database** window select the Table for data entry

2 Choose **AutoForm** from the **New Object** list

3 A simple form is displayed on the screen.

4 Use **[Tab]** and **[Shift]-[Tab]** to move between fields (or point and click with the mouse).

5 At each field key in the required data.

6 When you reach the last field, **[Tab]** takes you to the first field in the next record.

Take note

When you enter data through a form, it is recorded in the associated table. If you opt not to save the form, the data is still saved.

68

Basic steps

Naming your Form

1 Click the **Save** tool 💾

or

if you have closed the Form without saving, click `Yes` at the **Save changes** prompt.

2 At the **Save As** dialog box give the form a name. This can be any length and contain several words, eg *Contacts Simple Form*

3 Click `OK`

❑ The form will be listed on the **Forms Tab** of the Database Window.

When you have keyed in all the data, you will want to return to your Database window. Save and name the form before you go. You will be prompted to do this if you try to close without saving.

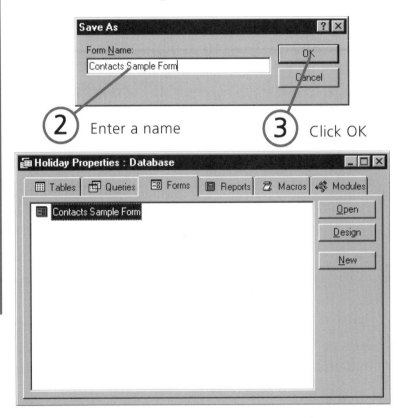

Enter a name

Click OK

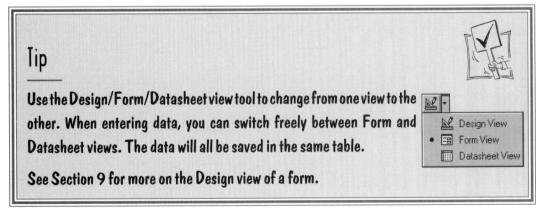

Tip

Use the Design/Form/Datasheet view tool to change from one view to the other. When entering data, you can switch freely between **Form** and **Datasheet** views. The data will all be saved in the same table.

See Section 9 for more on the Design view of a form.

69

Summary

❑ To **open a database**, click the **Open Database** icon on the toolbar and complete the dialog box as required

❑ To **open a table** in **Datasheet view**, select the Tables tab on the Database window, then double click the table name

❑ To **move between fields** in your datasheet use [Tab] or [Shift]-[Tab], the mouse or the keyboard shortcuts

❑ To **move between records** use the arrows on the left of the status bar, or the scroll bars and the mouse, or the keyboard shortcuts

❑ To **go to a specific record** press [F5], key in the record number and press [Enter]

❑ To display your **records in a form layout**, choose **Autoform** from the New Object list.

❑ To **change your view** use the **View** tool

❑ The **contents of a field**, can be edited, replaced or deleted during initial data entry or at any later time

❑ To **add a record** to your table, click the New Record tool on the toolbar, then key in the detail

❑ To **delete a record**, select it, then press [Delete]

6 Redesigning a table

Adding a field 72

Deleting a field 74

Changing field properties 75

Primary key and indexes 76

Summary 78

Adding a field

New fields can easily be added to an existing table. Try adding two fields to the *Accommodation* table.

● *Town* has the Text data type, and will fit above *Country*.

● *Star Rating* will go above *ContactID*. This field should have the Number data type and an Integer format. Add a Validation Rule set to accept only a 1 or 2 or 3 or 4 (our star rating system).

● If you are working through the project, make up some *Town* and *Star Rating* details.

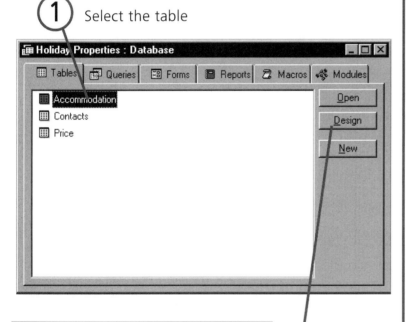

(1) Select the table

(2) Click Design

Take note

To add a field at the end of your field list, simply scroll down to the first empty row, and key in the details required.

1 At the **Database** window, select the table whose design you want to edit

2 Click [Design]

3 Select the row (field) that you want to have below the new one

4 Click the **Insert Row** tool

A new field is added *above* the selected one

5 Key in the detail - field name, data type, description, and set the field properties

6 Add other fields as required

7 Save the changes - click the **Save** tool

8 Close the Design window by clicking its close button

72

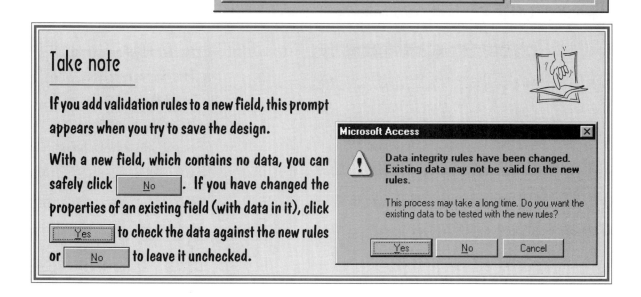

3 Select a row

Accommodation : Table

Field Name	Data Type	Description
⛌ Reference	AutoNumber	
Season Start	Date/Time	Only needed if not open all year
Season End	Date/Time	Only needed if not open all year
▶ Country	Text	
Type of Accommodation	Text	Enter C, F, A or R
Board	Text	Enter HB, SC or BB

Field Properties

General | Lookup

Field Size	20
Format	
Input Mask	
Caption	
Default Value	
Validation Rule	
Validation Text	
Required	No
Allow Zero Length	No
Indexed	Yes (D

A field name can

8 Close

Accommodation : Table

Field Name	Data Type	Description
⛌ Reference	AutoNumber	
Season Start	Date/Time	Only needed if not open all year
Season End	Date/Time	Only needed if not open all year
▶		
Country	Text	
Type of Accommodation	Text	Enter C, F, A or R

Field Properties

General | Lookup

A field name can
be up to 64
characters long,
including spaces.
Press F1 for help
on field names.

5 Key in details

Take note

If you add validation rules to a new field, this prompt appears when you try to save the design.

With a new field, which contains no data, you can safely click [No]. If you have changed the properties of an existing field (with data in it), click [Yes] to check the data against the new rules or [No] to leave it unchecked.

Microsoft Access ⚠

Data integrity rules have been changed.
Existing data may not be valid for the new rules.

This process may take a long time. Do you want the existing data to be tested with the new rules?

[Yes] [No] [Cancel]

73

Deleting a field

Redundant fields are just as easily removed. Any data held within a field which you delete is permanently erased - so be careful with this one!

Basic steps

1 Open the table in Design view (see page 72)

2 Select the row (field) that you want to delete

3 Click the **Delete Row** tool

4 Confirm the deletion at the prompt

5 Save the changes

6 Close the Design window

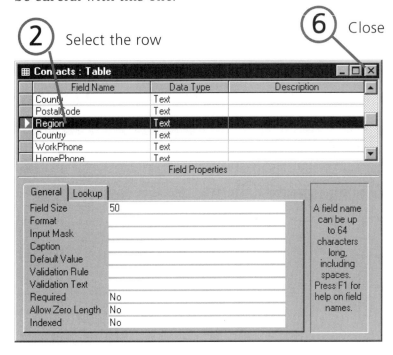

(2) Select the row

(6) Close

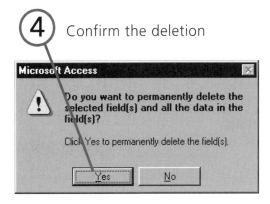

(4) Confirm the deletion

Tip

Before deleting a field, go into Datasheet view and check the field contents. If it contains some data in any record, think twice before you delete .

Changing field properties

Field properties can also be modified as required. In the *Price* table, we can change the field properties of the fields with a **Currency** data type, to show 0 decimal places.

1 Open the table in Design view

2 Select the first field with a **Currency** data type

3 Press **[F6]** to move to the lower pane

4 Drop down the **Decimal Places** list and change the property to 0

5 Do this for all the fields with the Currency data type

6 Save your changes and close the Design window

(1) Open the table in Design view

(2) Select the field

(6) Close

	Field Name	Data Type	Description	
🔑	Price Range	Text	Price category A-E	
▶	Jan-Feb	Currency		
	Mar-Apr	Currency		
	May-Jun	Currency		
	Jul-Aug	Currency		
	Sept-Oct	Currency		

Price : Table

Field Properties

General | Lookup

		The number of digits to the right of the decimal separator. Select "Auto" if you want the format to determine
Format	Currency	
Decimal Places		
Input Mask	Auto	
Caption	0	
Default Value	1	
Validation Rule	2	
Validation Text	3	
Required	4	
Indexed	5	
	6	

(3) Press [F6]

(4) Select the new property from the list

Tip

If you accidentally delete a field or change its properties, then change your mind, close the table without saving the changes. When you reopen it, the field (and its contents) will still be there as before.

Primary key and indexes

You may decide that the field that you originally set as your Primary Key, is no longer appropriate.

Changing the Primary Key is simply a case of setting a new one. (*See page 43*)

If you want to remove Primary Key status from a field, and **not** set a new one, you must use the **Indexes** dialog box.

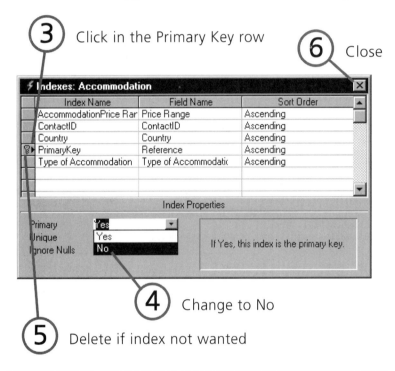

③ Click in the Primary Key row

⑥ Close

④ Change to No

⑤ Delete if index not wanted

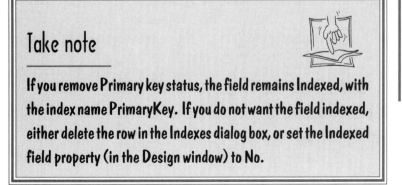

Take note

If you remove Primary key status, the field remains Indexed, with the index name PrimaryKey. If you do not want the field indexed, either delete the row in the Indexes dialog box, or set the Indexed field property (in the Design window) to No.

1 Open a table in Design view (use any table to try this out)

2 In Design view, click the **Indexes** tool 📇
or
Choose **Indexes** from the **View** menu

3 In the **Indexes** dialog box, position the insertion point in the **Primary Key** index entry

4 Change **Primary** to **No** (or click the Primary Key tool) – the Primary Key status is removed

5 To remove a field from the Indexes list, select the row and press **[Delete]**

6 Click the **Indexes** tool again to close the dialog box (or click the Close button)

(Set your primary key again if necessary)

Basic steps

1 Open the *Accommodation* table in Design view

2 Move the insertion point to the *Town* field

3 Press **[F6]** to go to the lower pane

4 Set the *Indexed* field to *Yes (Duplicates OK)*

5 Do the same with the *Star Rating* field

6 Save the changes

7 Close the table

 Press [F6]

Tip

To see a list of the Indexed fields in your table, press 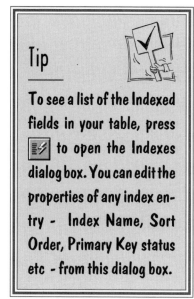 to open the Indexes dialog box. You can edit the properties of any index entry - Index Name, Sort Order, Primary Key status etc - from this dialog box.

Adjusting indexes

Fields can be indexed at the initial design stage, or during a later edit of the design.

You should index those fields you will want to sort on or search on, as it speeds up sorting and searching.

In the *Accommodation* table, we could index the *Town* and *Star Rating* fields, as we might want to sort our accommodation on town or star rating order, or search for all accommodation in certain towns or with specific star ratings.

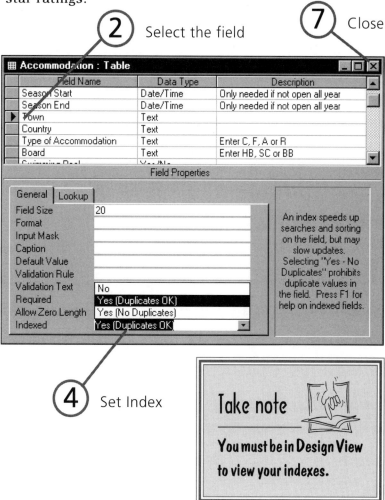

Select the field

Close

Set Index

Take note

You must be in Design View to view your indexes.

Summary

❑ To **add a field in the middle** of your table, select the field that will be below your new field and click the **Add Row** tool on the Toolbar

❑ To **add a field to the end** of your field list, simply scroll down to the end of the list and key in the new field details

❑ To **delete a field**, select the row, then click the Delete Row tool on the toolbar

❑ **Field Properties** are easily changed - position the insertion point in the field, press [F6] to move to the lower pane, make the changes, then press [F6] to return to the upper pane

❑ To **Remove Primary Key** status from a field, and not set another field as the primary key, you must go into the Indexes dialog box

❑ Fields that are likely to be sorted or searched on should be **Indexed**

❑ Remember to **Save** your edited Design

7 Datasheet display

Gridlines 80

Hiding columns 81

Showing columns 82

Fonts 83

Heights and widths 84

Freezing columns 85

Print Preview 86

Page Setup 88

Printing your table 89

Summary 90

Gridlines

So far, we have been content with the way our tables appear on the screen. However, depending on the number of fields in your table, and what you want to look at, you may need to change the format of your datasheet.

You can also print data out from your table in Datasheet view, so you might want to consider customising the datasheet format before you print (covered later in this section).

By default, the gridlines are displayed between the rows and columns of your table. Most of the time this is what you want, but, particularly if you are going to print your table in Datasheet view, you might prefer to switch them off. Viewing and hiding gridlines is an on/off toggle - you switch them on and off using the same command.

It is assumed the gridlines are displayed at this stage.

Basic steps

1 Open the **Format** menu

2 Click **Cells...**

3 Complete the **Cells Effects** dialog box as required

4 Click OK

Take note

If you make the Gridline colour the same as the background colour, your gridlines are "hidden".

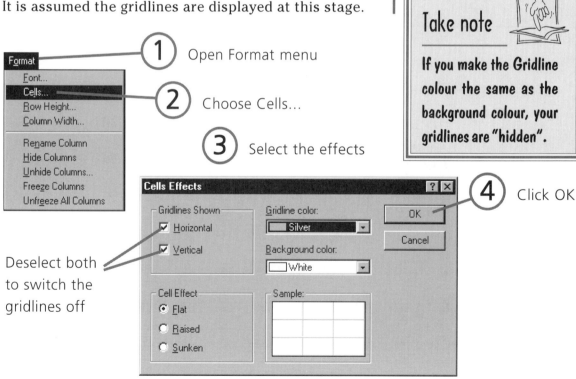

① Open Format menu

② Choose Cells...

③ Select the effects

④ Click OK

Deselect both to switch the gridlines off

80

Basic steps

1 Select the column(s) you want to hide

❏ To select a column, click in the field name row at the top

❏ To select adjacent columns, click and drag along the field name row

2 Choose **Hide Columns** from the **Format** menu

You may not want all the columns in your table to be visible. You may be concentrating on a task that only uses certain fields and decide to hide the ones that are of no concern at the moment, or you might want to print out only certain columns from your datasheet.

① Select columns

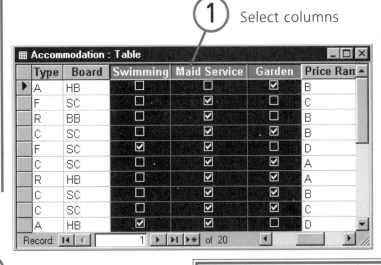

Choose Format – Hide Columns

Columns hidden

Take note

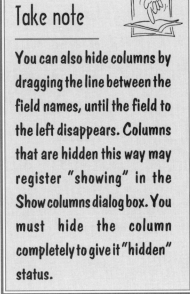

You can also hide columns by dragging the line between the field names, until the field to the left disappears. Columns that are hidden this way may register "showing" in the Show columns dialog box. You must hide the column completely to give it "hidden" status.

Showing columns

If you have hidden some columns, there will come a time when you need to show them again. The easiest way to reveal hidden columns is to use the Unhide Columns command in the Format menu.

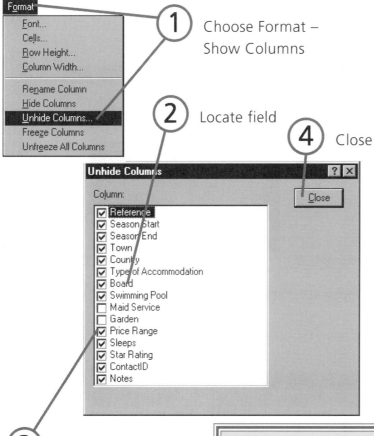

Choose Format –
Show Columns

Locate field

Close

Tick to Show,
clear to hide

Basic steps

1 Open the **Format** menu and choose **Unhide Columns**

❑ The **Unhide columns** dialog box appears. The Columns currently showing have a tick beside them.

2 Scroll up and down the list to locate the field name you want

3 Toggle the show/hide status by selecting the field you wish to show, or deselecting those you wish to hide

4 When you have specified which fields to show, and which to hide, click [Close]

Take note

You can "show" hidden columns by dragging, but it can be tricky! Locating the column border in the field name row (where one border overlays another when columns are hidden) can be a frustrating exercise using the mouse!

Basic steps

1 Choose **Font...** from the **Format** menu

2 In the **Font** dialog box, select the font, size and style

❏ The **Sample** area shows the effect your selections will have on the characters

3 Click [OK] to return to the datasheet with your new settings

Take note

When you change the font, it changes it for the whole datasheet, not just the column(s) or row(s) you have selected.

The default character style (font) is Arial, 10 point. You may want to change the font style or size if you have been formatting your datasheet with a view to printing it. You might want to use a larger font, or make the print bold for example.

You can change the font style and/or size by using the **Font** dialog box.

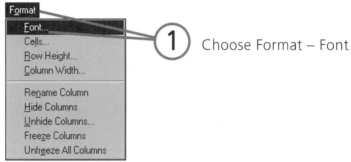

Choose Format – Font

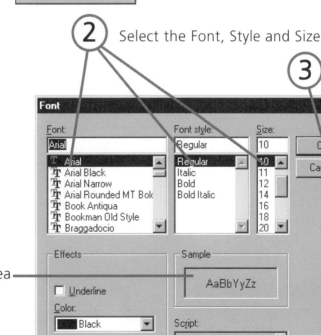

Select the Font, Style and Size

Click OK

Sample area

Heights and widths

You can change the **Row Height** for all the records in your datasheet. You might need to do this if you have chosen a Font that does not fit into the current row height. Height is measured in *Points*, the same as Fonts sizes.

The **Column Widths** are initially determined by the field size or the field name size that appears at the top of each column. You can change the displayed width when in Datasheet view. Width is measured in characters.

Basic steps

- ❏ **Setting the Row Height**
- **1** Choose **Row Height...** from the **Format** menu
- **2** Set the height – or check the Standard Height box.
- **3** Click [OK]
- ❏ **Setting the Column Width**
- **1** Select the column(s) to change
- **2** Choose **Column Width...** from the **Format** menu
- **3** Set the required width
- **4** Click [OK]

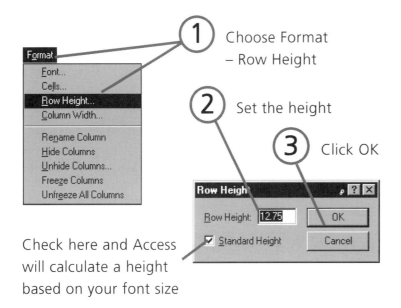

① Choose Format – Row Height

② Set the height

③ Click OK

Check here and Access will calculate a height based on your font size

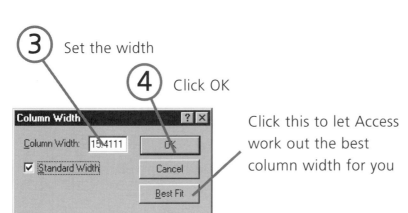

③ Set the width

④ Click OK

Click this to let Access work out the best column width for you

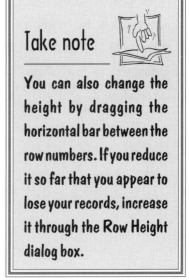

Take note

You can also change the height by dragging the horizontal bar between the row numbers. If you reduce it so far that you appear to lose your records, increase it through the **Row Height** dialog box.

84

Freezing columns

1 Select the column(s) you want to Freeze

2 Choose **Freeze Columns** from the **Format** menu

3 The selected column(s) are Frozen at the left of the table. If you choose columns that are not at the left, they will be moved there when you give this command.

❑ To unfreeze your columns, choose **Unfreeze All Columns** from the **Format** menu

There will be times that you will need to view columns that are distant from each other in the table, on the screen at the same time . This can be done by hiding (see page 81) or by **freezing** columns at the left hand side of your screen. They will remain in position, while the other columns can be scrolled in and out of sight as necessary.

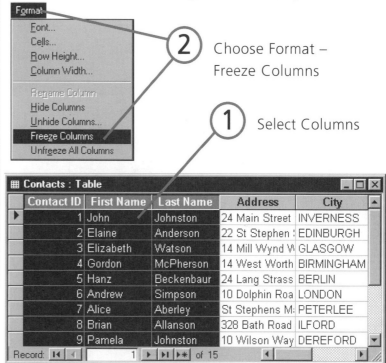

② Choose Format – Freeze Columns

① Select Columns

Thick line separates Frozen from other columns

Take note

If you Freeze columns, with no gridline display, a thick line appears to the right of the frozen columns.

Print Preview

Now that you have some data in your table(s), you will most likely want to print it out at some stage. There are various ways of doing this, but an easy way to begin with is to print from Datasheet view.

Once the datasheet display has been formatted to your satisfaction, you can print the table.

Do a Print Preview first, and check that the layout is okay on screen, before you commit it to paper.

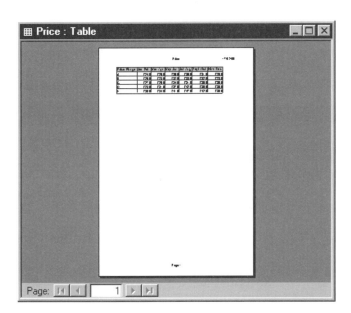

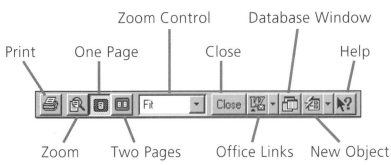

Print   One Page   Zoom Control   Close   Database Window   Help

Zoom   Two Pages   Office Links   New Object

Basic steps

1 Open the table you want to print in Datasheet view

2 Format it as required (see pages 80 to 85)

3 Click the **Print Preview** tool

❑ Your table is displayed in the Print Preview screen.

Take note

There is a special toolbar in Print Preview. You can use the tools to send your table to the printer, zoom in on your document or out from it, or close the Preview window and return to your table in Datasheet view.

86

Basic steps

Zoom

1 Move your mouse pointer over the area of the table you want to zoom in on (notice that the mouse pointer looks like a magnifying glass)

2 Click the left mouse button

3 You are zoomed in, so you can read the data (you might need to use the scroll bars to see areas not displayed on the screen)

4 Click the left button again to zoom out

❑ The **Zoom** icon 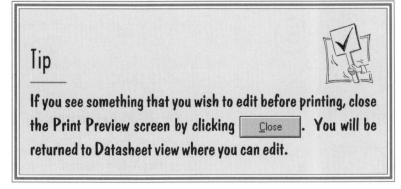 acts as a zoom in/ zoom out toggle too.

In Print Preview, it is very difficult (if not impossible) to read the data being displayed. This is not usually a problem, as you are really just checking the presentation of the data, not the detail. However, if you do want to check an entry, you can Zoom in to get a better look!

You cannot edit the data from the Print Preview screen – if you notice something is inaccurate or you want to change the formatting of the table, you must close Print Preview and return to the datasheet to make the changes.

Price Range	Jan-Feb	Mar-Apr	May-Jun	Jul-Aug
A	£240	£260	£300	£350
B	£260	£280	£320	£380
C	£275	£296	£340	£310
D	£285	£310	£370	£420
E	£300	£340	£410	£470

Zooming in lets you check details of the layout

Tip

If you see something that you wish to edit before printing, close the Print Preview screen by clicking `Close`. You will be returned to Datasheet view where you can edit.

Page Setup

If you need to change the margins or orientation of your page, you can use the Page Setup dialog box to make the necessary changes. You can get to it from the Print Preview screen or from Datasheet view.

Basic steps

1 Open the **File** menu and select **Page Setup**

2 Complete the **Page Setup** dialog box as required

3 Click [OK]

❑ You will be returned to Print Preview

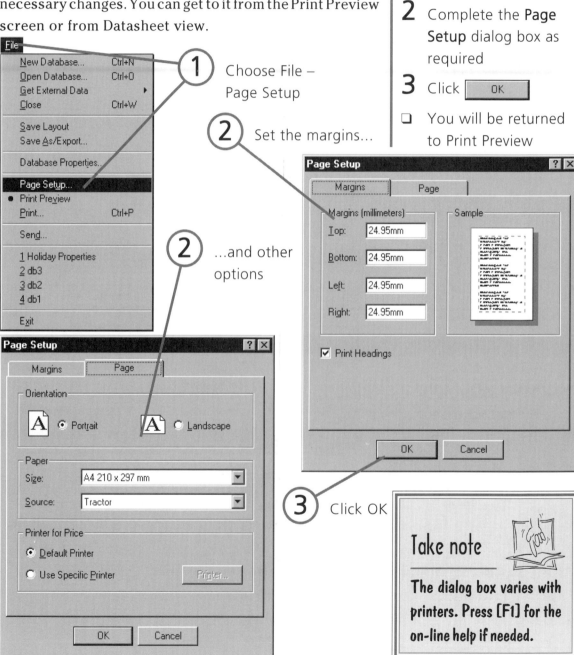

Choose File – Page Setup

Set the margins...

...and other options

Click OK

Take note

The dialog box varies with printers. Press [F1] for the on-line help if needed.

Basic steps

1 If you only want to print certain records, select them now

2 Choose **Print** from the **File** menu

3 Complete the **Print** dialog box as required

4 Click [OK]

Take note

To send your table directly to the printer, using the default print settings, click the Print tool 🖨.

Printing your table

If the table is formatted and the printer setup is okay, you can go ahead and print your table. You can print directly from Datasheet view, or from the Print Preview screen. Either way, the routine is the same.

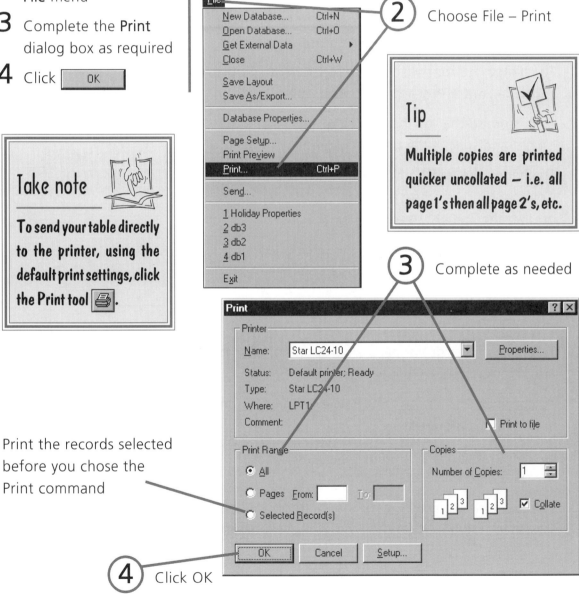

Choose File – Print

Tip

Multiple copies are printed quicker uncollated – i.e. all page 1's then all page 2's, etc.

Complete as needed

Print the records selected before you chose the Print command

Click OK

Summary

- ❏ The **Gridlines** can be changed from the Cells Effects dialog box

- ❏ To **hide columns**, select the columns then choose Format – Hide columns

- ❏ To **show hidden columns**, choose Format – Unhide Columns and complete the dialog box as required

- ❏ To **change the font** used in your datasheet, choose Format – Font and select from the options

- ❏ To **customise the row height**, choose Format – Row Height and specify the required height

- ❏ To **change the width of columns** choose Format – Column Width, and set the width in the dialog box, or drag the line between the field names

- ❏ To **stop columns scrolling** off the screen, select them and choose Format – Freeze columns

- ❏ To **unfreeze your columns**, choose Unfreeze all columns from the Format menu

- ❏ To **preview your datasheet** before printing, click the Print Preview tool on the toolbar

- ❏ To **check details** on the Print Preview screen, zoom in and out as required

- ❏ To **change the margins**, paper size or orientation of the paper, go into Page Setup

- ❏ To **print your datasheet**, click the Print tool on the Datasheet toolbar or on the Print Preview toolbar

8 Sorting and searching

Find 92

Filter by selection 93

Sort 94

Multi-level sorts 95

Saving queries 97

Multi-table queries 98

Setting the Query criteria 100

Reusing queries 102

Query Wizard 104

Summary 108

Find

With larger databases, it is impractical to locate records by scrolling through, reading each row. Instead, you can use the **Find** command, which will locate records that contain a specified item of text. Find works most efficiently if you know what field the data is in (so you don't need to search the whole table), and the field is *Indexed*.

③ Enter target data

④ Where in the field?

⑤ Up, down or all table?

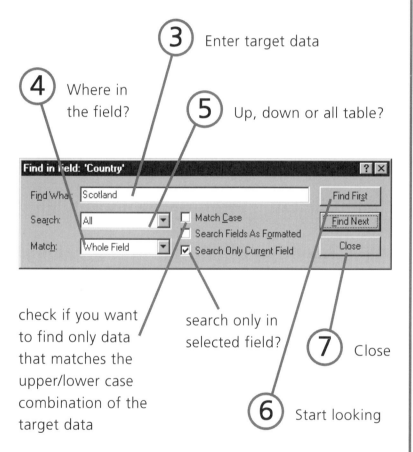

check if you want to find only data that matches the upper/lower case combination of the target data

search only in selected field?

⑦ Close

⑥ Start looking

Basic steps

1 If you know what field the data is in, position the insertion pointer in it before you start

2 Click the **Find** tool The **Find** dialog box appears. Drag on its title bar to move it so that does not obscure the data you are working with.

3 Key the target data in the **Find What:** slot

4 In **Match:** indicate where the data appears in the field

5 In **Search In** , specify whether to search the whole table, or up or down from the current record

6 Click [Find First] to start the search, or [Find Next] after you have found one and want the next match

7 When you have found all you want, click [Close]

Basic steps

1 Select the text you want to base your filter on, eg *Scotland* in the *Country* field

2 Click the **Filter by selection** tool 🦊

❏ Records matching the selection are displayed

3 Repeat the process if you want a sub-set of your new list eg only self-catering properties

❏ You can repeat the process until you are down to the records you want

4 Click the **Apply/ Remove filter** tool 🔽 to display all your records again.

When working within a table, you might want to display a subset of the records held based on some criteria eg all the properties in Scotland. You can use **Filter by selection** techniques for this.

② Select text in the field

▦ Accommodation : Table						
Reference	Season S	Season E	Town	Country	Type	
1			Inverness	Scotland	A	
2			Bath	England	F	
3	01/02/96	01/12/96	Cardiff	Wales	R	
4			Dublin	Ireland	C	
5	18/01/96	10/12/96	Aberdeen	Scotland	F	
6			Paris	France	C	
7			Hamburg	Germany	R	
8			Berlin	Germany	C	
9			Chaville	France	C	

Record: ◄◄ ◄ 1 ► ►◄ ►* of 20

The filtered sub-set is also sorted on the selected field

▦ Accommodation : Table							
Reference	Season S	Season E	Town	Country	Type	Board	Swimr
1			Inverness	Scotland	A	HB	☐
5	18/01/96	10/12/96	Aberdeen	Scotland	F	SC	☑
10			Glasgow	Scotland	A	HB	☑
13			Carrbridge	Scotland	F	SC	☐
* (AutoNumber)							☐

Record: ◄◄ ◄ 1 ► ►◄ ►* of 4 (Filtered)

93

Sort

When you key records into a table, they appear in the order they were input, or that of the primary key if one is set. There will be times when you need the records in a different order, ascending or descending, using some other field in the table. For example, in the *Accommodation* table, you might decide to re-arrange, or **sort**, your records into *Country*, *Town* or *Star Rating* order.

Sorting your records on one field is very easy. We could use the *Accommodation* table to try this out.

(1) Open the table

(2) Click in the field you want to sort on

Basic steps

1 Open the table you want to sort (in our case *Accommodation*)

2 Put the insertion point anywhere in the field you want to sort your records on

3 Click the Ascending Sort [A↓] or Descending Sort [Z↓] tool

❑ The records are re-arranged as indicated

Accommodation : Table

Reference	Country	Type	Board	Swimming	Maid Service
1	Scotland	A	HB	☐	☐
2	England	F	SC	☐	☑
3	Wales	R	BB	☐	☑
4	Ireland	C	SC	☐	☑
5	Scotland	F	SC	☑	☑
6	France	C	SC	☐	☑
7	Germany	R	HB	☐	☑
8	Germany	C	SC	☐	☑
9	France	C	SC	☐	☑
10	Scotland	A	HB	☑	☑
11	England	F	SC	☑	☑
12	Wales	A	BB	☑	☐
13	Scotland	F	SC	☐	☑
14	Italy	C	SC	☑	☑
15	Spain	A	SC	☑	☑

Record: |◄ ◄ 3 ► ►| ►* of 20

Take note

You can be anywhere, in any row, in the field you want to sort on. The whole table will be sorted in the requested order (ascending or descending) of the data in that field.

Multi-level sorts

If you need to sort your table on more than one field, you have to set the sort up as a **Query**. Multi-level sorts are very useful, when for example, you have a table of clients and you want to sort the records by *Country*, then by *City*, then by *Company*. These take longer than one field sorts, and the more levels you sort to, the longer it takes.

We'll do a simple multi-level sort, rearranging the records in the *Accommodation* table by *Country*, then by *Town*.

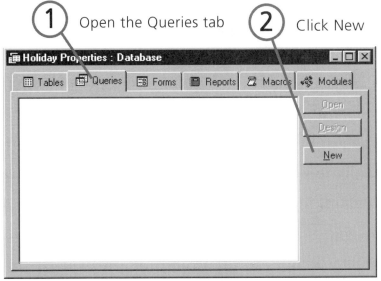

① Open the Queries tab ② Click New

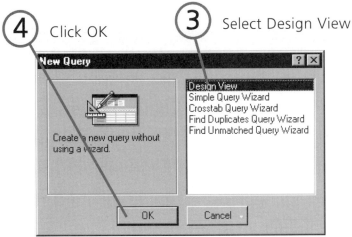

④ Click OK ③ Select Design View

1 Select the **Queries** tab at the Database window

2 Click [New]

3 Select **Design View** at the **New Query** dialog box

4 Click [OK]

5 At the **Show Table** dialog box, select the table and click [Add]

6 Click [Close] to close the **Show Table** dialog box

7 Double click on each field required in the list to add it to the lower pane

8 Set the **Sort** for each field (drop down the list and pick *Ascending* or *Descending*)

9 Click the Run it tool [!]

❑ The sorted table is displayed

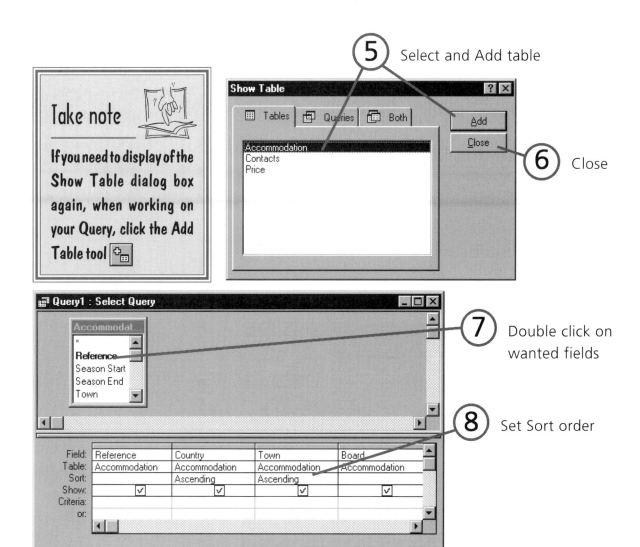

5 Select and Add table

6 Close

7 Double click on wanted fields

8 Set Sort order

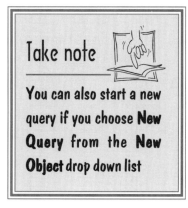

Take note

If you need to display of the Show Table dialog box again, when working on your Query, click the Add Table tool

Take note

You can also start a new query if you choose **New Query** from the **New Object** drop down list

Basic steps

1 Click the Save tool in either the design or result screen

2 At the **Save As Query** dialog box, enter a meaningful name for the sort – any length and having several words if you like

3 Click [OK]

❑ When you return to the **Database** window, you will find the Query located on the **Queries** Tab.

Your new query

Saving queries

If you have set up a complex sort, you might want to save it, so you can use it again.

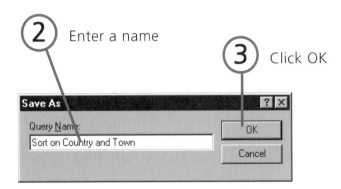

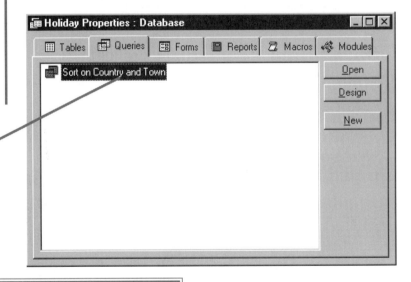

Take note

You can easily move from the Design View to Datasheet View as you develop your query.

97

Multi-table queries

If you have more than one table in your database, there will come a time when you need to interrogate several tables at the same time in order to locate the information you require. To do this in Access you set up a **Query**.

This example draws data from three tables. I want to find properties that sleep more than 4, and for each matching property, I want details of:-

● what Town the property is in (*Accommodation*)

● the Contact's name and phone number (*Contacts*)

● the cost of the property in May/June (*Price*)

You can build up a Query from the Database window.

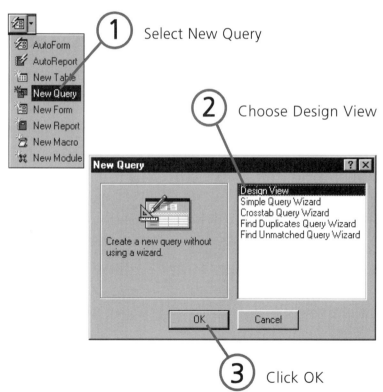

① Select New Query

② Choose Design View

③ Click OK

❑ **Adding the tables**

1 Pick **New Query** from the **New Object** list

or

1 Click [New] on the **Queries** tab

2 At the **New Query** dialog box, choose **Design View**

3 Click [OK]

❑ This opens the **Select Query** and **Show Table** dialog boxes, where you specify the tables you want to query and set up your criteria

❑ The **Show Table** dialog box should be open. If it is not, click the **Show Table** Icon 🔲

4 Select the table(s) that you want to query, one at a time. Click ┃ Add ┃ to add them to the **Select Query** dialog box

5 When all the tables have been added, click ┃ Close ┃ to close the **Show Table** dialog box.

④ Select a table and Add it

⑤ Close

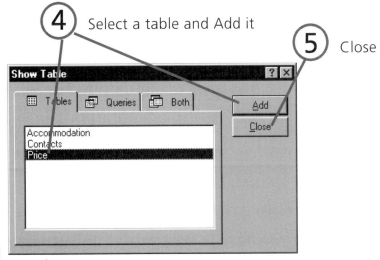

Join lines

In the upper half of the Select Query dialog box, the join-lines between the tables are displayed. These lines indicate the fields that relate one table to another. We can see that the *Accommodation* and *Contacts* tables are related through the *ContactID* field. The *Accommodation* table and the *Price* table are related through the *Price Range* field. The primary key in each table is displayed in bold type in the field list.

Selected tables and their join lines are shown in the upper pane

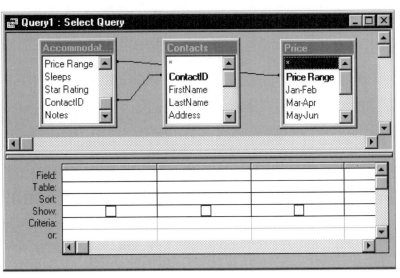

Setting the Query criteria

Basic steps

The next stage is to select fields to be included in the output, and to specify any criteria that are to be used to select records. We want the *Town* and *Sleeps* fields from *Accomodation*, with the criteria *>4* (more than 4) set for *Sleeps*; *FirstName, Last Name* and *HomePhone* from *Contacts*; and *May-Jun* from *Price*. If we set the **Sort** mode, we can also determine the order of records in the output.

Basic steps

1 Select fields for inclusion by double-clicking on them in their table lists.

2 Set the sort and/or selection criteria (if required)

3 If you do **not** want to display the field contents when you run the query, click the **Show** checkbox to remove the tick

① Double-click to select

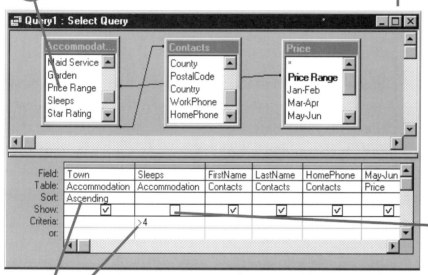

② Set sort or criteria

③ Clear check box if not wanted

Take note

When setting criteria you can use the relational operators:

>	more than	<	less than
=	equal to	<>	not equal to
>=	more than or equal to	<=	less than or equal to

These are mainly used in Number and Date/Time fields, but can be used with Text. >"H" means "after H in the alphabet"

4 Save the Query .

5 Give the Query a suitable name

6 Click [OK]

7 Apply the new Query by clicking the **Run It** tool ❗

8 Close the Query

❑ The result is shown as a table in Datasheet view

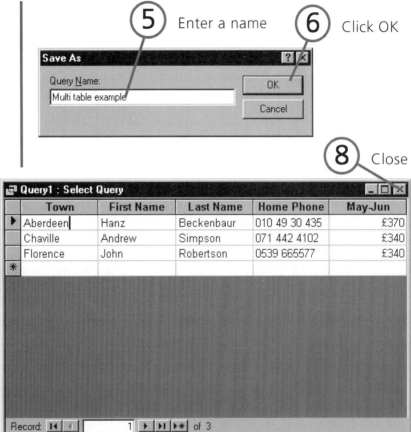

⑤ Enter a name   ⑥ Click OK

Save As

Query Name:
Multi table example

[OK]
[Cancel]

⑧ Close

Query1 : Select Query

Town	First Name	Last Name	Home Phone	May-Jun
Aberdeen	Hanz	Beckenbaur	010 49 30 435	£370
Chaville	Andrew	Simpson	071 442 4102	£340
Florence	John	Robertson	0539 665577	£340
*				

Record: |◄ ◄ 1 ► ►| ►＊ of 3

Take note

The Query can be found on the Queries Tab in the Database window

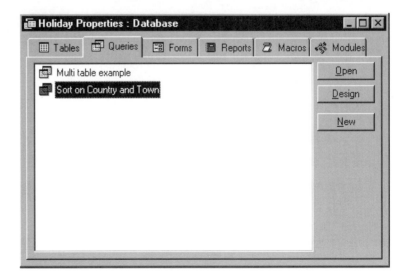

Holiday Properties : Database

| Tables | Queries | Forms | Reports | Macros | Modules |

Multi table example
Sort on Country and Town

[Open]
[Design]
[New]

101

Reusing queries

Sometimes you will want to rerun an existing query without alteration; sometimes you may want to make a minor adjustment to a query before reusing it; other times it is quicker to start from scratch with a new one.

Basic steps

1 Open the Database window

2 Select the **Queries** tab

3 Select the Query name

4 Click [Open]

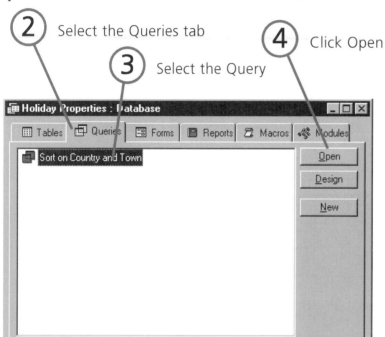

② Select the Queries tab

③ Select the Query

④ Click Open

❏ The table is opened, listing the records in the order set by the sort criteria, or the sub-set of records selected by a filter

Tip

You can double click the query name on the Queries tab to open the query and run it.

Sort on Country and Town : Select Query

Reference	Country	Town	Board	Price Range	Sleeps
2	England	Bath	SC	C	4
16	England	London	SC	C	2
11	England	York	SC	D	4
9	France	Chaville	SC	C	6
6	France	Paris	SC	A	4
20	France	Paris	BB	C	2
8	Germany	Berlin	SC	B	4
7	Germany	Hamburg	HB	A	2
19	Ireland	Cork	HB	D	2
4	Ireland	Dublin	SC	B	4
14	Italy	Florence	SC	C	6
18	Jersey	St Helier	SC	C	4
17	Orkney	Stromness	SC	B	4

Record: ◄◄ ◄ 1 ► ►► ►* of 20

Basic steps

1 Open the Database window

2 Select the **Queries** tab

3 Select the Query name

4 Click [Design]

5 At the **Select Query** dialog box check and update your sort or selection criteria as necessary.

6 **Save** the Query and/or Run it [!]

Editing a Query

Editing from the Database window is very similar to when setting up a new query - you're just not starting from scratch! New criteria may be added, and existing ones removed or changed.

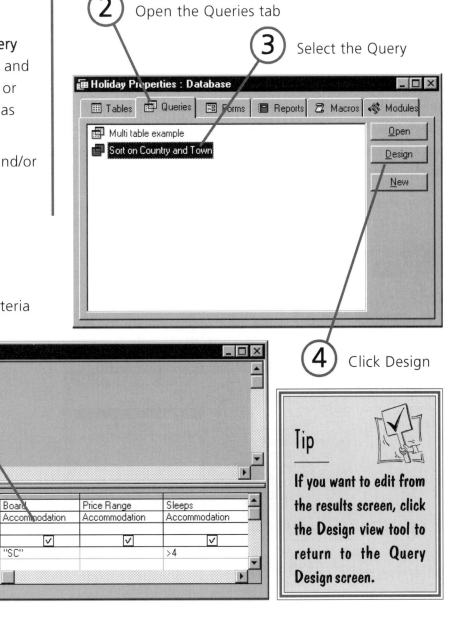

② Open the Queries tab

③ Select the Query

④ Click Design

⑤ Edit the criteria

Tip

If you want to edit from the results screen, click the Design view tool to return to the Query Design screen.

Query Wizard

When we were building up tables, we found there was a Table Wizard to help. There is also a Wizard to take you through the process of building up a query. With the Query Wizard, you'll find it provides a useful way of creating rather complex queries - queries that you might otherwise find difficult, if not impossible, to do without spending much more time learning Access.

To demonstrate the Query Wizard feature, we will build a query that will interrogate the Accommodation table to find out how many properties we have in each country. We then want to break down the total number of properties, so we can tell how many properties each contact has in each country.

To do this, we will use a Crosstab Query Wizard.

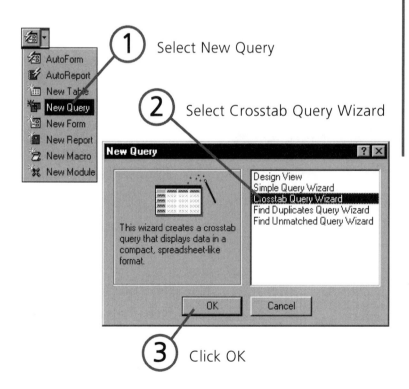

① Select New Query

② Select Crosstab Query Wizard

③ Click OK

1 Pick **New Query** from the **New Object** list

or

1 Click `New` on the **Queries** tab

2 Choose **Crosstab Query Wizard**

3 Click `OK`

Information required

We must now specify:-

❑ the tables or query to use

❑ the field(s) detail to display in each row

❑ the field to use for column headings

❑ the type of calculation required

Basic steps

1 Specify the table that has the detail we want in our result table (*Contacts* in our case)

2 Specify the field or fields you wish to use as row headings (*Country* in this example)

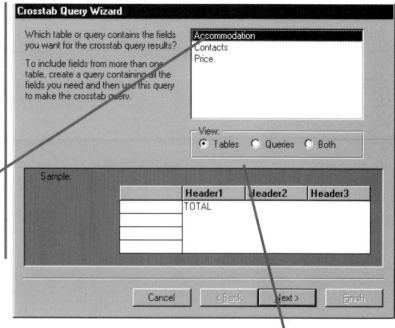

(1) Table to base results on

(2) Select fields for row headings

Do you want a list of tables, queries or both?

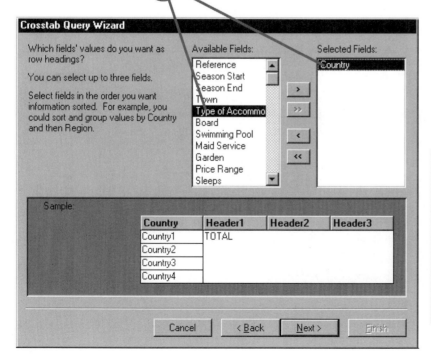

Take note

Remember to click `Next >` **after each step.**

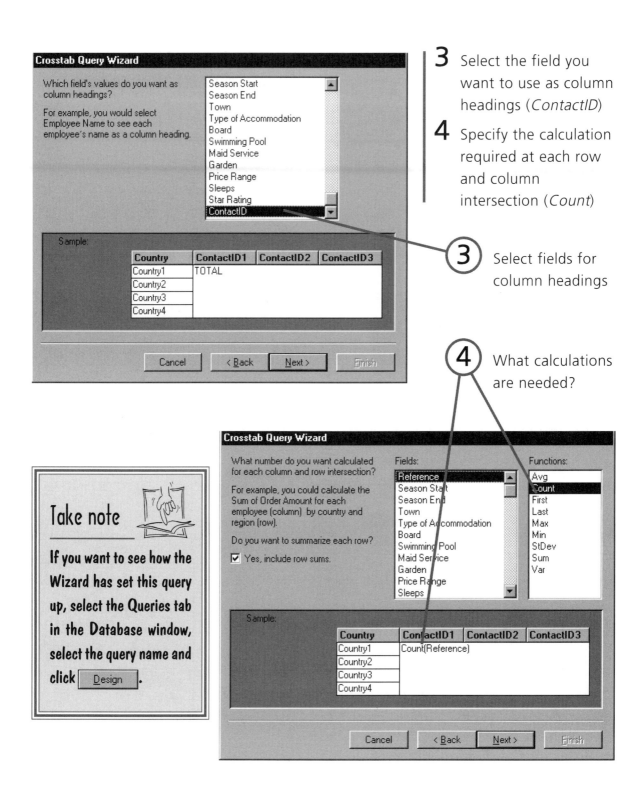

3 Select the field you want to use as column headings (*ContactID*)

4 Specify the calculation required at each row and column intersection (*Count*)

(3) Select fields for column headings

(4) What calculations are needed?

Take note

If you want to see how the Wizard has set this query up, select the Queries tab in the Database window, select the query name and click Design.

Basic steps

1 Name the query, either accept the suggested name or replace it with a more appropriate one

2 Choose what to do next, I suggest **View the query**

3 Click [Finish]

The output from the query, showing the calculated values

Finishing off

Okay, nearly there. You should be at the chequered flag!! All that's left to do is name the query and decide what to do next.

(1) Edit the name to suit

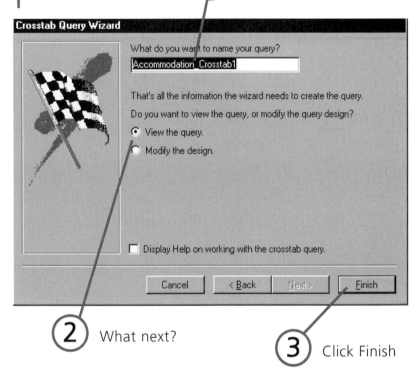

(2) What next?

(3) Click Finish

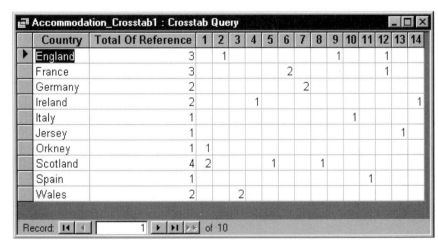

Country	Total Of Reference	1	2	3	4	5	6	7	8	9	10	11	12	13	14
England	3	1								1		1			
France	3						2					1			
Germany	2							2							
Ireland	2				1										1
Italy	1										1				
Jersey	1													1	
Orkney	1	1													
Scotland	4	2				1			1						
Spain	1											1			
Wales	2			2											

Record: |◄ ◄ [1] ► ►| ►* of 10

Summary

- ❏ If you know what data a field contains, you can use the **Find** command to locate it

- ❏ To **sort your records** into Ascending or Descending order, place the insertion point in the field you want to sort on, then click the appropriate Sort tool

- ❏ **Multi-level sorts** must be set up as a Query

- ❏ **Save** your Query if you wish to **reuse** it

- ❏ To **interrogate several tables** at the same time, you must set up a Query

- ❏ You can use a **Query Wizard** to set up a Query

9 Forms

Designing a form 110

Headers and footers 112

Adding fields 115

Save your form 116

Form view 117

Using Form Wizard 118

Summary .124

Designing a form

Forms allow you to customise your screen for input and editing purposes, making the screen more "user friendly".

We have already used a basic form generated by Autoform in Section 5. In this section we will design from scratch a simple form and a more ambitious one generated by a Form Wizard.

The first form displays name, telephone number and address details for our Contacts.

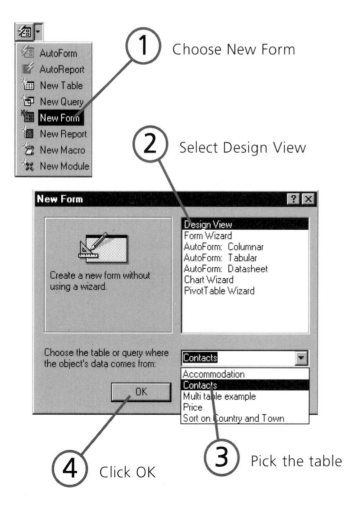

① Choose New Form

② Select Design View

③ Pick the table

④ Click OK

1 From the **Forms** tab in the **Database** window, click [New]

or

select **New Form** from the **New Object** drop down list

2 At the **New Form** dialog box, select **Design View**

3 Drop down the list of **Tables/Queries** and choose the Table or Query (*Contacts* in our case) that supplies data for the form

4 Click [OK]

❑ You arrive at the Form Design screen.

Take note

You can use the tools or the View menu options to change views and switch screen elements on or off. If your Toolbox or Field List are not displayed, open them now.

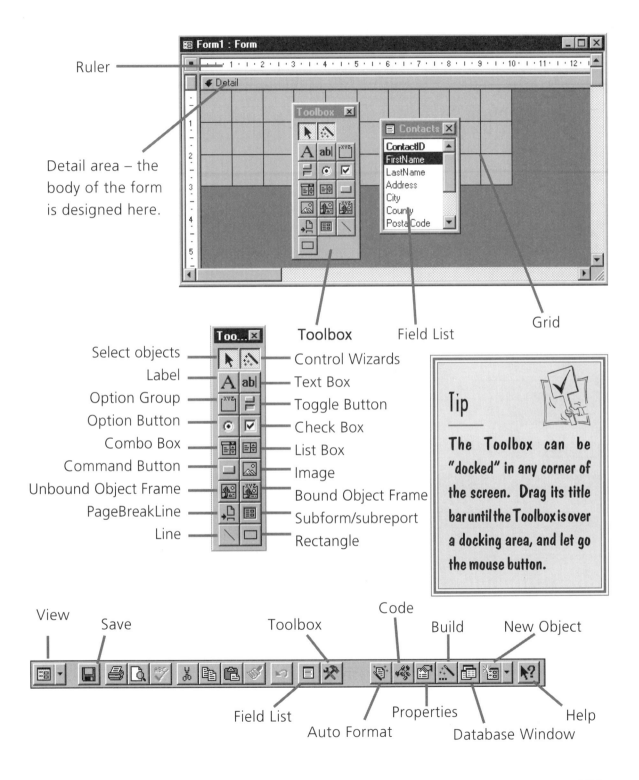

Ruler

Detail area – the body of the form is designed here.

Form1 : Form

◆ Detail

Toolbox

Contacts
ContactID
FirstName
LastName
Address
City
County
PostalCode

Toolbox   Field List   Grid

Select objects ─── Control Wizards
Label ─── Text Box
Option Group ─── Toggle Button
Option Button ─── Check Box
Combo Box ─── List Box
Command Button ─── Image
Unbound Object Frame ─── Bound Object Frame
PageBreakLine ─── Subform/subreport
Line ─── Rectangle

Tip

The Toolbox can be "docked" in any corner of the screen. Drag its title bar until the Toolbox is over a docking area, and let go the mouse button.

View   Save   Toolbox   Code   Build   New Object

Field List   Auto Format   Properties   Database Window   Help

Headers and footers

Usually, you will have some descriptive text in your form. The text may be a heading for your form, column headings, or some narrative with instructions to the user. In this example we want the form title and the column headings for our tabular layout. This text, which we will put in the Form header area, is called a **Label**.

We must display the **Form Header** and **Footer** areas first, then insert the labels.

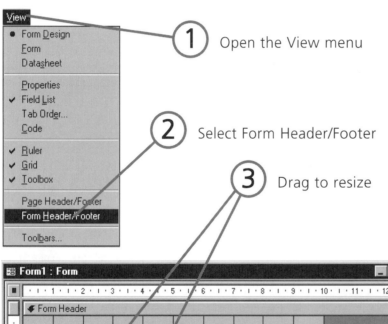

① Open the View menu

② Select Form Header/Footer

③ Drag to resize

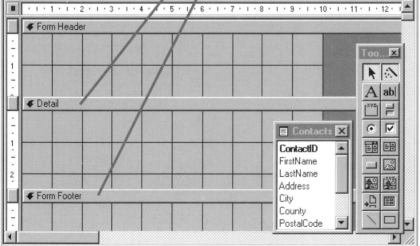

1 Open the **View** menu

2 Choose **Form Header/ Footer**

❑ A Header area appears above, and a Footer area appears below, the Detail area

3 Resize the Header and Footer areas by dragging the lower edge of the area, up or down (we need to increase the size of the Header and decrease the size of the footer – in fact make it disappear!)

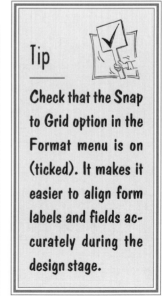

Tip

Check that the Snap to Grid option in the Format menu is on (ticked). It makes it easier to align form labels and fields accurately during the design stage.

Basic steps

1 Click the **Label** tool

2 Move the mouse pointer – now ⁺**A** – to where you want your first label

3 Click and drag to draw a rectangle

4 Type in your label text, e.g. *Property Contacts*

5 Repeat steps 1-4 for each column heading, e.g. *Details of Property Owners or Contacts*

Adding Labels

The headings we are going to put on our form are purely descriptive – they are not part of the table the form is designed around. We can therefore make the text anything we want. This can be very useful for instructions .

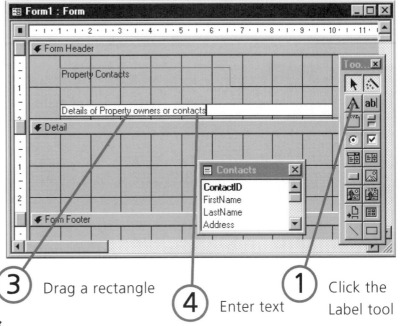

③ Drag a rectangle ④ Enter text ① Click the Label tool

Adjusting Design Elements

If you position a label (or any element) incorrectly or make it too big or small, this is easily amended. First select it by clicking anywhere on it. Note the handles that appear around the edges of a selected element.

To Resize	To Move	To Delete
1 Point to a handle. The pointer changes to a double headed arrow	1 Point to an edge (not a handle). The pointer changes to a hand	1 Press the [Delete] key
2 Drag the arrow to resize	2 Drag the element into position	

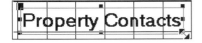 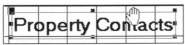 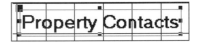

Formatting the labels

Now that your labels are on your form, in the correct postion and the correct size, you might want to enhance the appearance of them so they stand out clearly as headings. You might want to make them bigger, or bolder, or in italics – you choose!

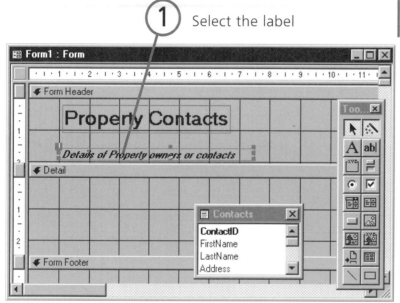

① Select the label

② Set the Font   ③ Set the Size

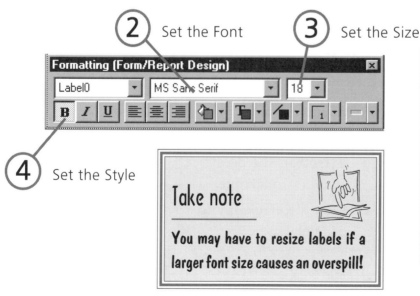

④ Set the Style

Take note

You may have to resize labels if a larger font size causes an overspill!

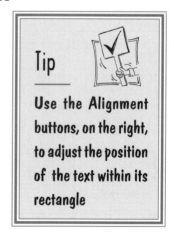

Tip

Use the Alignment buttons, on the right, to adjust the position of the text within its rectangle

114

Basic steps

1 Click the Field List tool 🔳 to display the **Field List**

2 Drag a field from the list (*Firstname*), and drop it in the Detail area

❑ *Both* components of the field are selected, but we want to deal with them separately

3 Click on the **field name** section to select it, and press **[Delete]**

4 If necessary, reposition and/or resize the field detail component

5 Repeat steps 2-4 for each field (*LastName, Homephone, Workphone, Address,* etc.) you require

❑ See page 117 for the final form layout.

We now need to position the fields we require in the Detail area of the form. This is done by simply clicking and dragging the required field from the field list to its destination on the form. When a field is dragged over however, it has two components – one for the field name and one for the field detail.

You can leave both parts on your form – or you could delete the field name part (as in this example) and use a Label to describe the data.

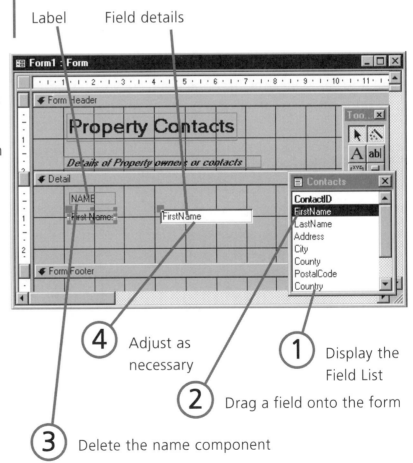

Label   Field details

④ Adjust as necessary

③ Delete the name component

② Drag a field onto the form

① Display the Field List

Save your form

Obviously, you need to save your form design if you want to keep it. You can save your design at any time – you don't need to wait until you have set the whole thing up. If you are designing a complex form, save it regularly.

Save and Save As/Export ...

If you have already saved your form, and have edited the design since the last save, use **File - Save**, or click 🖫 to replace the old version of the form with the new one.

If you want to save the edited version as a separate form, you must use **File - Save As/Export...** to give it a different name. This can be very useful if you are designing several similar forms – once the first one is saved, you can edit it to produce the next then save it with a different name.

Basic steps

1 Use **File – Save** or click the **Save** tool 🖫

2 At the **Save As** dialog box, key in a name for your form

3 Click [OK]

❑ The name will appear on the **Forms** tab in the Database window

Take note

If a form has never been saved, whichever Save you use will take you to the Save As dialog box

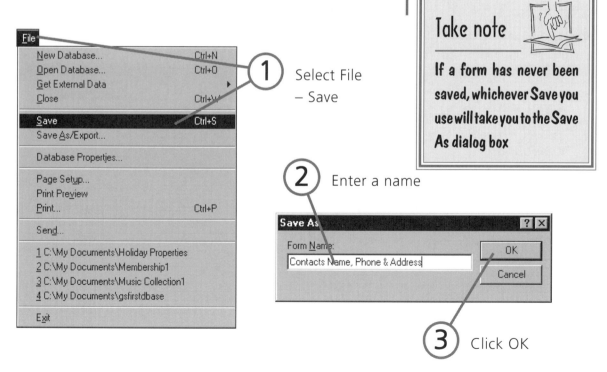

Select File – Save

Enter a name

Click OK

Basic steps

1 Click the **Form View** tool ![icon] or drop down the list and choose **Form View**

❏ The Form is displayed in Form view

2 Use **[Tab]** to move from field to field

3 Move between records using the forward and backward buttons

4 Click the **New Record** button if you wish to add another record

5 Close your form when you are finished

Let us look at our form in Form view, where one record will be displayed at a time on the screen. The layout of the form will be as you have designed in Design view.

It is assumed you are in the Form Design screen.

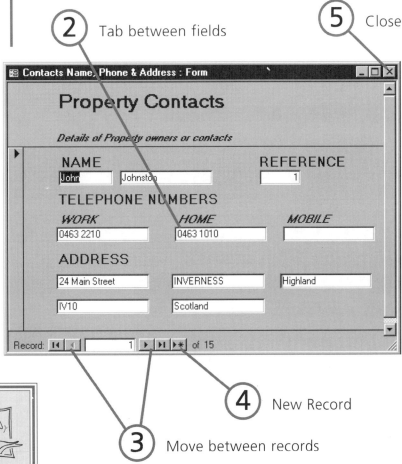

② Tab between fields

⑤ Close

Property Contacts

Details of Property owners or contacts

NAME | REFERENCE
John | Johnston | 1

TELEPHONE NUMBERS
WORK | *HOME* | *MOBILE*
0463 2210 | 0463 1010 |

ADDRESS
24 Main Street | INVERNESS | Highland
IV10 | Scotland

Record: 1 of 15

④ New Record

③ Move between records

Take note

If you are not happy with the look of the form, click the Design tool ![icon] to go back to Design view and edit it (remember to save any changes you make).

Using Form Wizard

We will use the Wizard to build a form that displays all the properties of a single owner. This project results in two forms being set up – a main form with details of the owner, and a sub-form with a list of the properties. The main form contains the sub-form and its details.

The Wizard must be told what fields to include from which tables. Here we need fields from the *Accommodation* table – *Type of Accommodation*, *Town* and *Price Range*; and from the *Contacts* table – *Firstname*, *Lastname* and *HomePhone*.

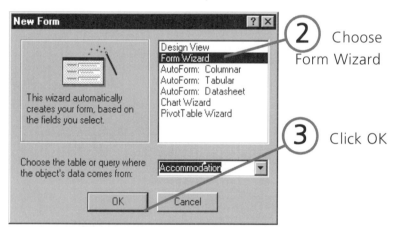

② Choose Form Wizard

③ Click OK

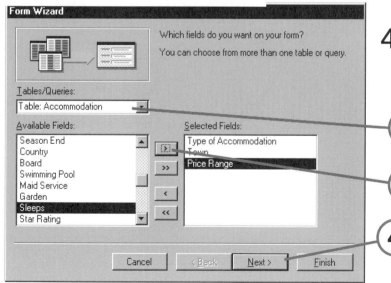

① Choose a table

② Add fields

④ Click Next

❏ **Choosing the Wizard**

1 From the **Forms** tab in the Database window, choose ⬚ New ⬚, or Click **New Form** on the **New Object** list

2 Select Form Wizard

3 Click ⬚ OK ⬚

❏ **Specifying the fields**

1 Select the first table – *Accommodation*

2 Add the desired fields from the **Available fields:** list, in the right order, to the **Selected Fields** list

3 Repeat for the *Contacts* table and its fields

4 Click ⬚ Next > ⬚

118

Basic steps

Selecting the Form Display options

1 Pick the **View** option required – choose **By Contacts** to achieve the same results as we have here

2 Select the **Layout** required for the sub-form – **Datasheet**

You must now specify what layout you want to use, the background style required and the name for the form or forms it creates – then Access takes care of the rest.

(1) Pick a View option

(2) Choose a layout

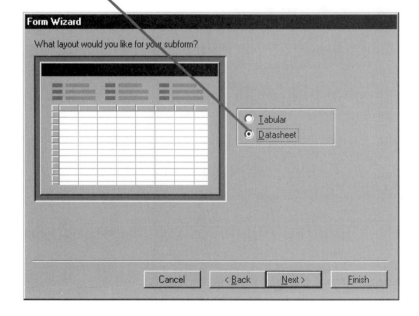

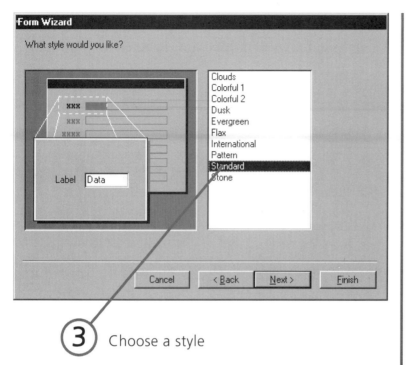

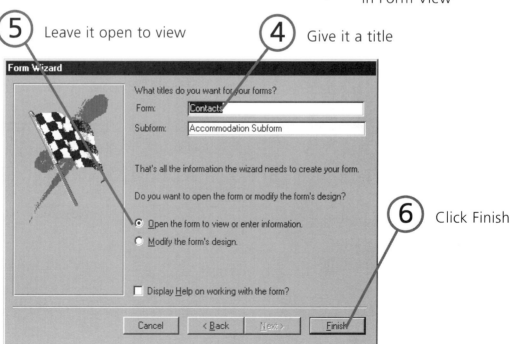

3 Choose the **Style** of form – this determines the background colour scheme and effects

4 Give your form (or forms) a Title – either accept the default, or type in a replacement

5 Leave the **Open the form to view or enter information** option selected

6 Click [Finish]

❑ Your Form is displayed in Form View

③ Choose a style

⑤ Leave it open to view   ④ Give it a title

⑥ Click Finish

The result

The new Contacts form is displayed. Each form gives the name and telephone of the property owner, together with a list of the properties he or she owns. Close your form to return to the Database window.

Subform

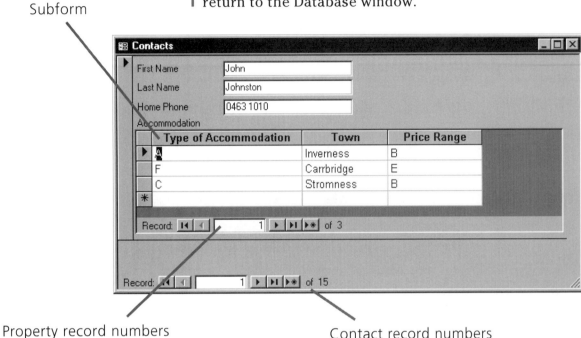

Property record numbers

Contact record numbers

❑ When you close your form, you will find two new forms listed on the Forms tab of the Database window.

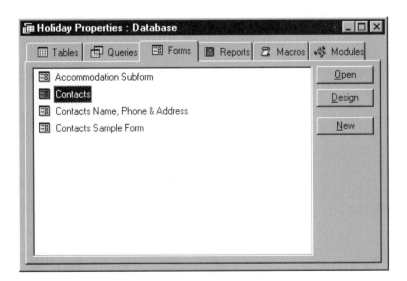

How did this happen?

It wasn't magic!! You could go into the Design view of each form to get an idea of what has happened behind the scenes.

Design view shows the *Accommodation Subform* to be very straightforward – just **Labels** in the **Form Header** area, and **Fields** from the *Accommodation* table in the **Detail** area – very similar to the first form we created in this section.

Labels in the Header

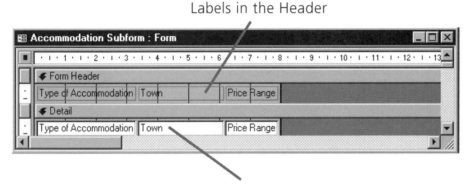

Design view of Accommodation Subform

Fields in the Details area

Design view for the *Contacts* form shows the **Form Header** area reduced to nothing, and fields (with both name and detail left in) in the **Detail** area together with the **Accommodation Subform** field.

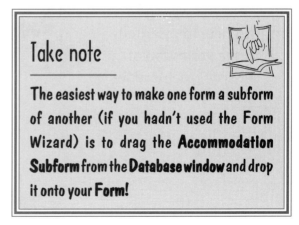

Take note

The easiest way to make one form a subform of another (if you hadn't used the Form Wizard) is to drag the **Accommodation Subform** from the **Database window** and drop it onto your **Form!**

Design view of Contacts form

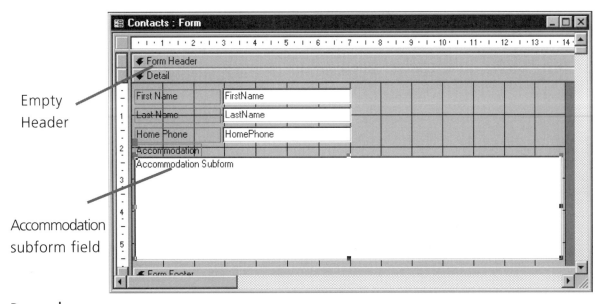

Empty
Header

Accommodation
subform field

Basic steps

1 Select the
Accommodation
Subform field

2 Click the Properties
tool 📝

3 Explore the **Properties**
dialog box

Checking the properties of a field

You can check the properties of the Accommodation
Subform field by opening its Properties dialog box.

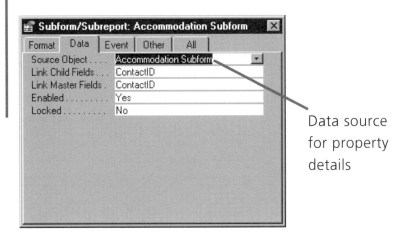

Data source
for property
details

Summary

❑ **Forms** allow you to customise your input and viewing screens

❑ Your **fields** can be placed anywhere on your form

❑ **Text** (for instructions and/or labels) can be included on your form to enhance its appearance and make it easier to use

❑ Forms can be designed from scratch using the Design view

❑ **Form Wizards** can help you design more complex forms using the information you give as the Wizard progresses

10 Reports

The Report design screen 126

Grouping records 128

Sorting grouped records 130

Adding a text box 131

Preview and print 132

Mailing labels 133

Summary 138

The Report design screen

Reports provide the most effective way of creating a printed copy of data extracted or calculated from the tables and queries in your database. They might be invoices, purchase orders, presentation materials or mailing labels.

Many of the features used in forms design are also used in report design. There are also a number of features that are unique to the Report environment. We will build our first report from scratch, and base it on the *Accommodation* table.

Basic steps

1 Click [New] on the **Reports** tab in the Database window or select **New Report** from the New Object list

2 At the **New Report** dialog box, select **Design view**

3 Choose the table on which you wish to base your report

4 Click [OK]

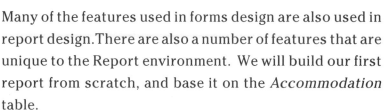

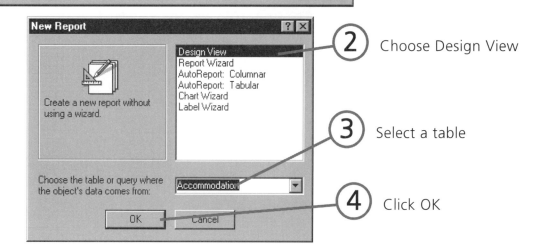

① Click New

② Choose Design View

③ Select a table

④ Click OK

Basic steps

1 Use the **Label** tool A to insert a field for the Page Header

2 Key in a suitable header eg "*LIST OF ACCOMMODATION BY STAR-RATING*"

3 Select the header and format it

4 Double click the **Line** tool ◤ to lock it on, then draw lines above and below the header.

5 Click the Pointer tool and select both lines

6 Select the border width required

7 Drag the lower edge of the **Detail** area up to give a sensible row height for our list

8 Click the **Field list** tool ▤ to display the list

9 Drag the required fields (eg *Country*, *Town*, *Board*, *Sleeps* and *Price*) into place on your report

Setting up the Page Header and Detail area

The techniques used here are very similar to those used in Forms design at this stage.

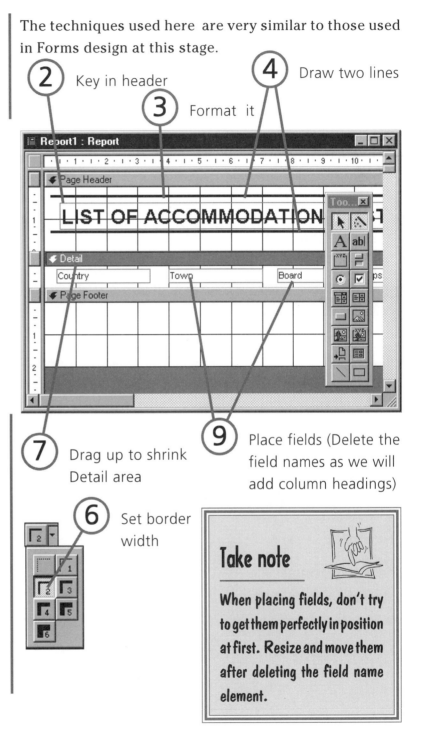

② Key in header

③ Format it

④ Draw two lines

⑦ Drag up to shrink Detail area

⑨ Place fields (Delete the field names as we will add column headings)

⑥ Set border width

Take note

When placing fields, don't try to get them perfectly in position at first. Resize and move them after deleting the field name element.

127

Grouping records

The records in our report are going to be grouped, so all the accommodation with a 1-star rating is together, all that with a 2-star rating is together and so on.

The Sorting and Grouping icon on the Toolbar is used to group your records.

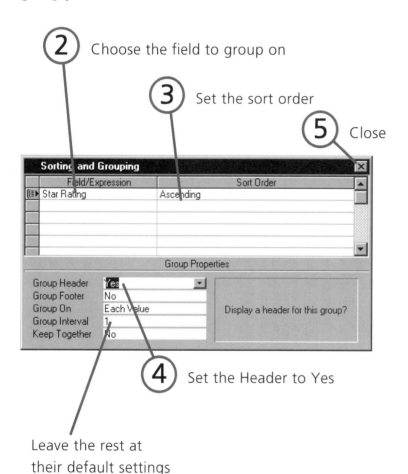

② Choose the field to group on

③ Set the sort order

⑤ Close

④ Set the Header to Yes

Leave the rest at
their default settings

1 Click the **Sorting and Grouping** tool

2 In the **Field/Expression** column, choose the *Star Rating* field from the list (this is the field on which we are going to group our records)

3 The **Sort Order** should be **Ascending** - to give 1-star to 4-star

4 Set the **Group Header** field to **Yes** – this will display a header area for our group

5 Close the **Sorting and Grouping** dialog box

Take note

The Sorting and Grouping tool is a toggle - you can use it to open and close the Sorting and Grouping dialog box.

Basic steps

1 Click and drag the *Star Rating* field over into the **Star Rating Header** area

2 Format the label and detail area of the field as required, e.g. bold, larger font, italics etc

3 Use the Label tool [A] to set up the column headings; key in the column headings required and format as you wish

Take note

You might need to resize or move your column headings in the Star Rating header area, and the fields in the detail area to get them all to line up.

Designing the Group Header area

We are going to have our grouped records preceded by a heading in the header area:- *Star-Rating 1*, *Star-Rating 2*, *Star-Rating 3*, *Star-Rating 4*

In addition to the group heading, we will put the column headings for the detail in here too.

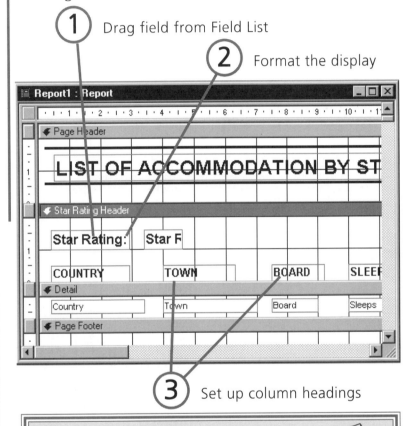

① Drag field from Field List

② Format the display

③ Set up column headings

Tip

To format several fields or labels in the same way (e.g. the column headings) select them all, using the [Shift]-Click method, then apply the formatting. This is usually quicker than doing each one individually.

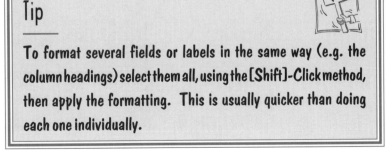

Sorting grouped records

We must now to specify how we want our records sorted within each *Star Rating* group. In this example, the main sort field within the group will be *Country*, and then *Town*. We must therefore tell Access to group our fields by *Star Rating*, and sort that field into Ascending order. Within each group, the records have to be sorted into ascending order based on *Country*, and within each Country, the records have to be sorted into ascending order on *Town*.

②　Select field and set sort order

④　Close

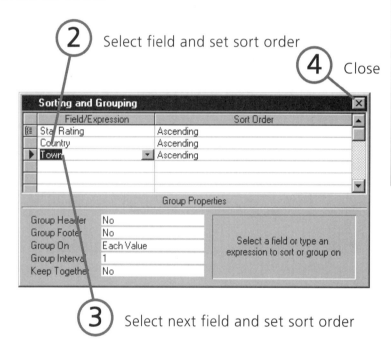

③　Select next field and set sort order

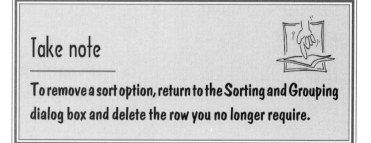

Take note

To remove a sort option, return to the Sorting and Grouping dialog box and delete the row you no longer require.

Basic steps

1 Click the **Text Box** tool, abl then click in the **Page Footer** area to place the Text Box

2 Delete the Field name and reposition the detail section if necessary

3 Select the detail section

4 Click the **Properties** tool 🖺 to open the **Properties** dialog box

5 In the **Control Source** field key in =*Now()* This expression returns the current date and time from your system

6 Close the Properties dialog box

7 Left align ▤ the Text Box so it lines up at the left margin of your report (the data will align to the right by default)

We are now ready to design the Footer area of our report. We will insert an Text Box here, where we can display the date and time of producing the report.

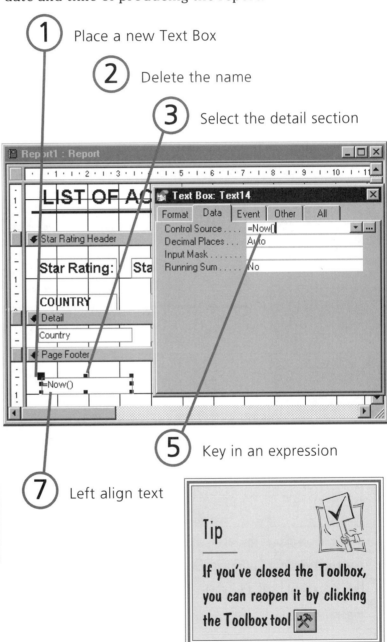

① Place a new Text Box

② Delete the name

③ Select the detail section

⑤ Key in an expression

⑦ Left align text

Tip

If you've closed the Toolbox, you can reopen it by clicking the Toolbox tool 🛠

Preview and print

You can now Print Preview your report, and print out a hard copy if you wish. There are two Preview choices here. The **Layout Preview** will give you a quick preview using sample data; the **Print Preview** takes longer to produce, but gives you a preview of the whole report.

 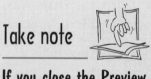
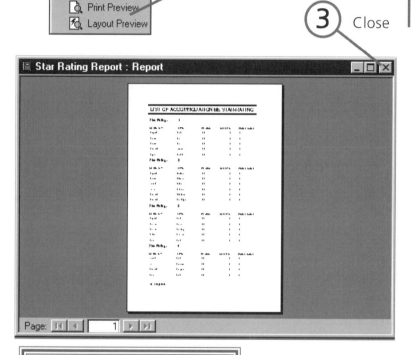

Select a Preview

Close

Take note

If you close the Preview window using the Close tool on the toolbar, you are returned to the Report Design screen. If you close the Preview window by clicking the close button, you are returned to the Database window.

Tip

Don't forget to save the report if you want to keep it for future use. Click the Save tool and give your report a name.

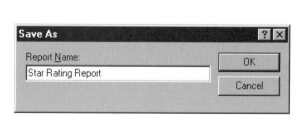

Basic steps

1. Click [New] on the **Reports** tab on the **Database** window, or choose **New Report** on the **New Object** list

2. Select **Label Wizard**

3. Choose the table on which you wish to base your mailing labels (*Contacts*)

4. Click [OK]

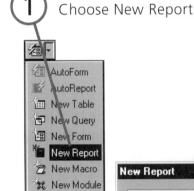

① Choose New Report

Mailing labels

This time, we will create a report to print Mailing Labels. We will use a Report Wizard, to take us through the steps required to generate them.

The mailing labels are for the owners we have for each property in our database. The name and address details required for the labels are in our Contacts table.

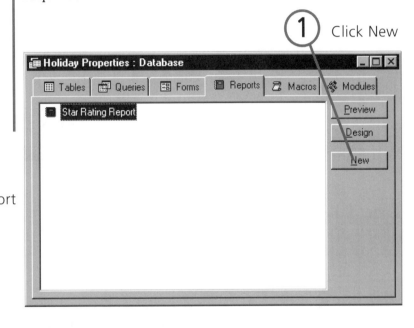

① Click New

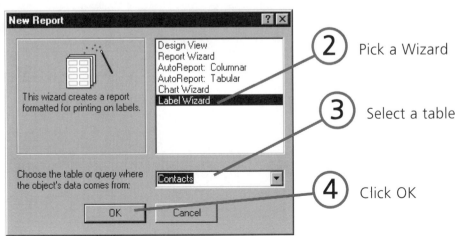

② Pick a Wizard

③ Select a table

④ Click OK

Specifying the Label Design

The next stage is to specify the layout. Getting data to fit comfortably on labels can be a tricky business, so check how they will look – and edit the design if necessary – before you print.

1 Choose the label size and the label type

2 Set the **Unit of Measure** to suit your labels

3 Modify the font style, size, attributes and colour as required

4 Build up the Label using the fields, text and punctuation,as required

5 If you want your labels printed in any specific order, specify the field to sort on

① Choose label size and type

② Unit of Measure?

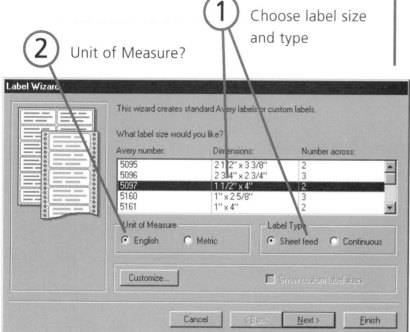

③ Set font and style options

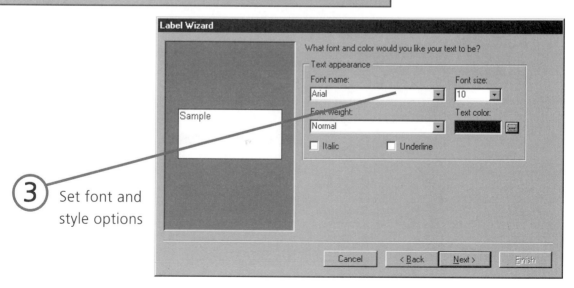

134

6 Edit the Report name

7 Choose **See the mailing labels as they will look printed**

8 Click [Finish]

④ Create the label

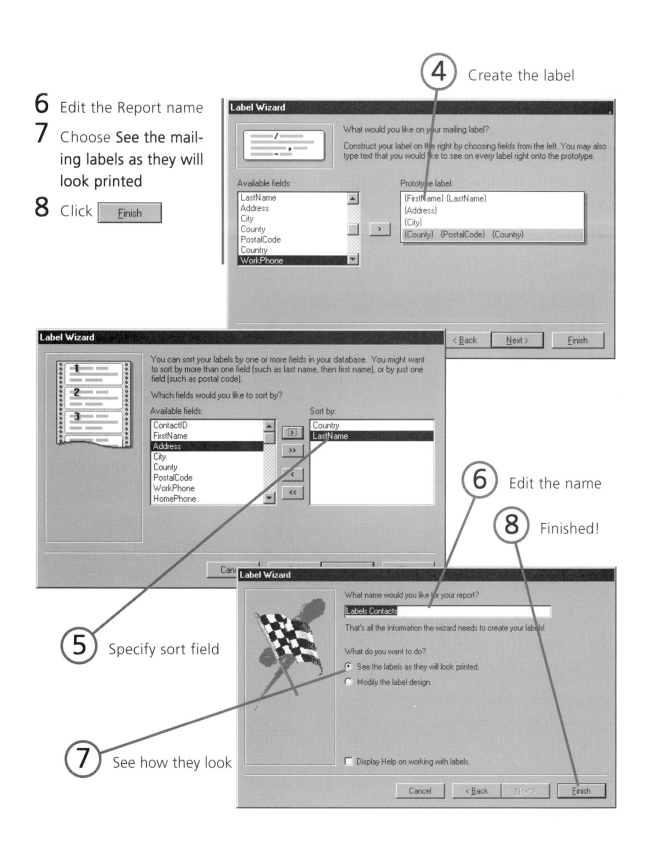

⑤ Specify sort field

⑥ Edit the name

⑧ Finished!

⑦ See how they look

Editing the Design

The labels are displayed in Print Preview. You can use the Page Setup to modify margins and orientation if necessary, or click the Print tool to print your labels out.

If you want to modify the design of your labels, or save the label report for future use, you must return to Design view by clicking Close on the Print Preview toolbar.

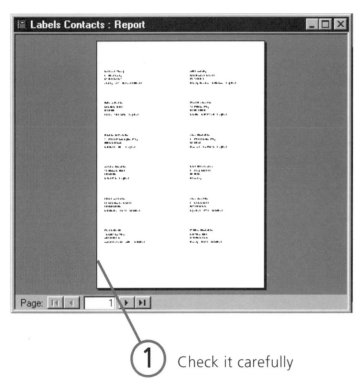

① Check it carefully

The Print Preview here shows us that we could have used a larger font without running out of space.

1 Check the **Print Preview** to see what needs to be done

2 Click [Close] to leave the **Print Preview** screen

❑ You are returned to the **Design** screen for the Mailing Labels

3 Use any of the Design features available to modify the design of your label

4 Click the **Save** tool 🖫 to Save the label design

5 Give the report a suitable name

6 Click [OK]

7 Click the Print tool  to print the labels if required

8 Close the Report

❑ You are returned to the **Reports** tab in the **Database** window. Your new report should be listed.

⑧ Close

Labels Contacts : Report

◆ Detail

=Trim([FirstName] & " " & [LastName])
=Trim([Address])
=Trim([City])
=Trim([County] & "   " & [PostalCode] & "   " & [Country])

③ Modify as required

New report listed

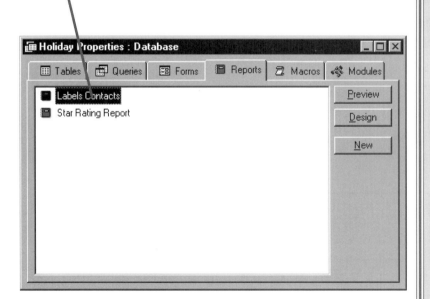

Holiday Properties : Database

| Tables | Queries | Forms | Reports | Macros | Modules |

Labels Contacts
Star Rating Report

Preview
Design
New

Take note

The **=Trim** code removes spaces to the right of the data in the field. This is very useful for address labels, where you want the fields on one line neatly closed up together and not spread out.

Look in the Properties dialog box for one of the fields to see the syntax of this command.

Summary

❏ Reports provide an effective way of presenting data extracted or calculated from your queries and tables

❏ Many of the **Forms design techniques** are also used in Report design

❏ Records can be **grouped and sorted** in your reports

❏ **Text Boxes** can be used to insert dates and times into your report

❏ You can use a **Wizard** to simplify the printing of Mailing Labels

Appendices

Database Wizard 140

A Accommodation table 144

B Contacts table 145

C Price table 146

Database Wizard

In addition to creating a database from scratch, as we have done in this book, you could use a Database Wizard to help you set up your tables, forms and reports.

There are several ready made databases that you can modify easily using the Wizard. Have a look through them to see if any could be useful to you.

Basic steps

1 Click the **New Database** tool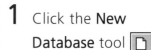

2 Select the **Databases** tab

3 Pick a database

4 Click OK

5 Name and create your database as shown in Section 3.

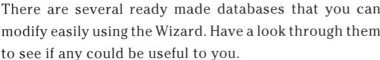

② Select the Databases tab

③ Choose a database

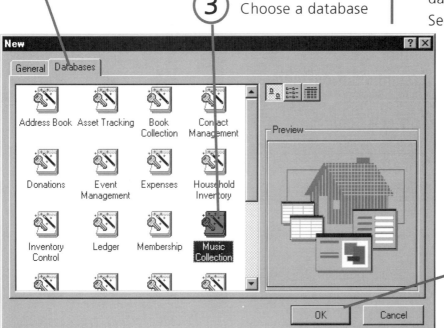

④ Click OK

Take note

The databases have full sets of fields, and predesigned forms and reports. The Wizard simply helps you to modify them.

Basic steps

❑ **Adding fields**

1 Click [Next >] at the introductory dialog box

2 Select a table

3 Tick those optional fields (shown in italics) that you would like to include

4 Repeat steps 2 and 3 for all tables.

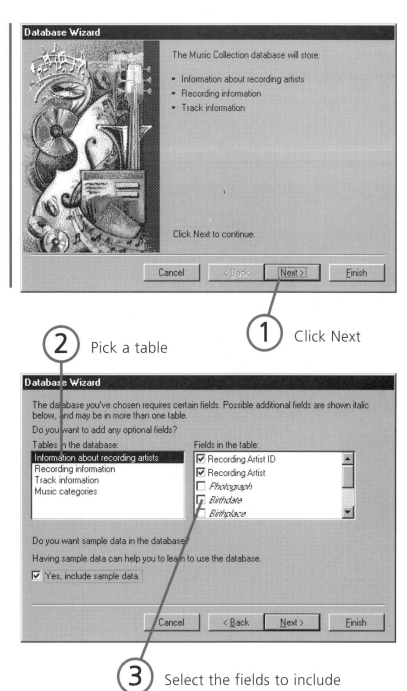

① Click Next

② Pick a table

③ Select the fields to include

Take note

Select the Yes, include sample data check box if you want some data set up to practice on

Setting the style

The next steps in the wizard let you select options that control the screen display and the printed reports. There are several options to choose from - browse through them until you find something you like.

The preview shows how it will look

1 Select a style for the screen display

2 At the next stage choose a style for your printed reports in the same way

3 Give your database a title

4 Tick the **Yes, I'd like to include a picture** box if you want a picture on each report

5 Click Picture... and select the picture from your disk

① Select a style

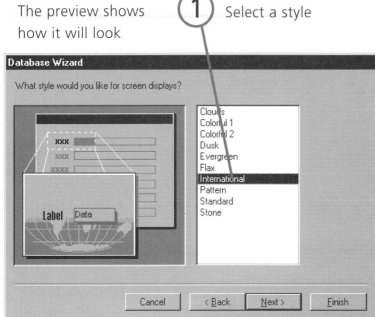

③ Enter a title

The picture could be your firm's logo, or just a decoration

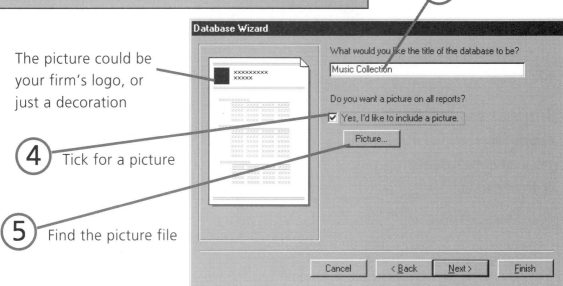

④ Tick for a picture

⑤ Find the picture file

6 If you want to start work on the database straight away, select **Yes, start the database** at the final step

7 Click [Finish], then wait while the Wizard creates your database

6 Start work?   **7** Finish

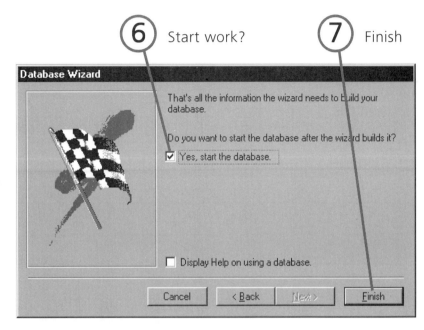

The Switchboard

This acts as a "front end" to your database, giving easy access to your forms and reports. Some options on the Main Switchboard – Enter/View Other Information and Preview Reports – lead to other Switchboards.

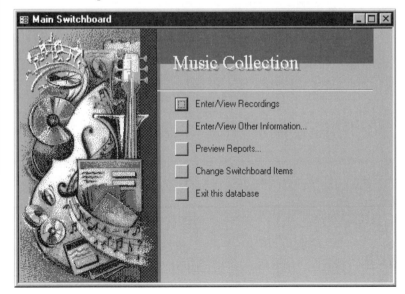

Take note

If the wizards produce tables, forms and reports that suit your needs then they can save you a lot of time by doing the ground work for you.

A Accommodation table

Ref	Season Start	Season End	Type of Accomm.	Country	Board	Swimming Pool	Maid Service	Garden	Price Range	Sleeps	Contact ID
1			A	Scotland	HB	No	No	Yes	B	4	1
2			F	England	SC	No	Yes	No	C	4	2
3	01/02/95	01/12/95	R	Wales	BB	No	Yes	No	B	2	3
4			C	Ireland	SC	No	Yes	No	B	4	4
5	18/01/95	10/12/95	F	Scotland	SC	Yes	Yes	No	D	6	5
6			C	France	SC	No	Yes	Yes	C	6	6
7			R	Germany	HB	No	Yes	Yes	A	2	7
8			C	Germany	SC	No	Yes	Yes	B	4	7
9			C	France	SC	No	Yes	Yes	C	6	6
10			A	Scotland	HB	Yes	Yes	No	D	4	8
11			F	England	SC	Yes	Yes	No	D	4	9
12			A	Wales	BB	Yes	No	Yes	E	4	3
13			F	Scotland	SC	No	Yes	No	E	4	1
14			C	Italy	SC	Yes	Yes	Yes	C	6	10
15			A	Spain	SC	Yes	Yes	No	D	4	11
16			C	England	SC	No	Yes	Yes	C	4	2
17			R	France	BB	No	Yes	Yes	C	2	12
18			C	Orkney	SC	No	Yes	Yes	B	4	1
19			A	Jersey	SC	Yes	Yes	Yes	C	4	13
20			R	Ireland	HB	Yes	Yes	Yes	D	2	14

ContactID	FirstName	LastName	Address	City	County	Postal Code	Country	Work Phone	Home Phone
1	John	Johnston	24 Main Street	INVERNESS	Highland	IV10	Scotland	0463 2210	0463 1010
2	Elaine	Anderson	22 St Stephen Street	EDINBURGH	Midlothian	EH110	Scotland	031 442 1021	031 556 0212
3	Elizabeth	Watson	14 Mill Wynd West	GLASGOW	Strathclyde	G13	Scotland	041 665 1043	041 510 5103
4	Gordon	McPherson	14 Worthington Way	BIRMINGHAM	Midlands	B24	England	021 557 9321	021 676 1999
5	Hanz	Beckenbaur	24 Lang Strasse	BERLIN			Germany	010 49 30 121	010 49 30 435
6	Andrew	Simpson	10 Dolphin Road	LONDON		N18 2WS	England	081 475 1010	071 442 4102
7	Alice	Aberley	St Stephens Manse	PETERLEE	Co Durham	SR8 5AJ	England	091 575 3928	091 653 1843
8	Brian	Allanson	328 Bath Road	ILFORD	Essex	1G2 6PN	England	081 543 6758	071 544 1234
9	Pamela	Johnston	10 Wilson Way	DEREFORD	Norfolk	NR19 1JG	England	0362 331112	0362 574098
10	Joan	Robertson	24 West Linton Way	KENDAL	Cumbria	LA9 6EH	England	0539 561732	0539 665577
11	William	Flux	132 London Road	CARNO	Montgomery	SY17 5LU	Wales	0686 203956	0686 105619
12	Amanda	Wilson	14 High Way	LAMPETER	Dyfed	SA4 8NW	Wales	0570 30651	0570 61234
13	William	Robertson	Hill View Rise	STROMNESS	Orkney	OK10	Scotland	0856 103212	0856 114322
14	Suzanne	Young	24 Causeway St	CLEMENT	Jersey	J21	Channel Is	0534 14261	0534 66310
15	Paul	Mitchell	45 Hill Top View	ABERDEEN	Aberdeenshire	AB24	Scotland	0224 10231	0224 54123

C Price table

Price Range	Jan-Feb	Mar-Apr	May-Jun	Jul-Aug	Sep-Oct	Nov-Dec
A	£240	£260	£300	£350	£310	£260
B	£260	£280	£320	£380	£320	£280
C	£275	£296	£340	£310	£360	£300
D	£285	£310	£370	£420	£390	£350
E	£300	£340	£410	£470	£425	£395

Index

A

Access Objects 4
Access screen 9
Add field 72
Add Record 66
Answer Wizard 20
Autoform 68

B

Blank Database 24

C

Close Database 59
Column Widths 84
Columns
    Freeze/Unfreeze 85
    Hiding 81
    Showing 82
Creating a new database 24
Creating a new table 26

D

Data Type
    Autonumber 30
    Currency 48
    Date/time 33
    Memo 42
    Number 40
    Text 36
    Yes/No 38
Database 59
    Close 59
    Create 24
    Open 62

Datasheet

    Data Entry 64
    Editing Data 65
    Fonts 83
    Moving within 64, 65
    Open 63
    Print 89
    View 63
Delete field 74
Delete Record 67

E

Edit record
    Add 66
    Delete 67
    Field contents 65
Exiting Access 9

F

Field List 111
Field names 6
Field Property
    Caption 31
    Default value 39
    Edit 75
    Field size 31
    Format 31, 33
    Indexed 31
    Input Mask 34
    New Values 31
    Required 41
    Validation Rule 37
    Validation Text 37
Field size 7
Filter by selection 93
Find 92

Form 4
  Adding fields 115
  Design View 110
  Field properties 123
  Formatting design elements 114
  Headers and footers 112
  Sub-form 118
  Wizard 118
Form view 117
Format
  Cells 80
  Fonts 83
Freeze Columns 85

G

Getting into Access 8
Gridlines 80
Grouping Records 128

H

Help
  Answer Wizard 20
  Contents tab 12
  Find tab 18
  Help tool 15
  Index tab 16
  Tooltips 15
Hiding columns 81

I

Indexes
  Edit 77
Indexes dialog box 76

K

Keyboard shortcuts 66

L

Label
  Form 113
  Mailing 133

M

Mailing labels 133

N

New
  Database 24
  Form 110
  Query 95
  Report 126
  Table 26

O

Objects 4

P

Page Setup 88
Primary Key 43, 55
  Remove 76
Print
  Datasheet 89
  Report 132
Print Preview 86

Q

Query 4
  Criteria 100
  Crosstab 104
  Design view 95
  Edit 103
  Hide field contents 100
  Multi-level sort 95